Daffodils and Pink Tulips

Poems & Random Reminiscenes

Richard Alan Bunch

Copyright © 2016 by Richard Alan Bunch

ISBN 978-1-4958-0994-1

Published July 2016

INFINITY PUBLISHING
1094 New DeHaven Street, Suite 100
West Conshohocken, PA 19428-2713
Toll-free (877) BUY BOOK
Local Phone (610) 941-9999
Fax (610) 941-9959
Info@buybooksontheweb.com
www.buybooksontheweb.com

To the memory of my parents and sister

and to

Rita, Katharine, and Rick

With best wishes

Richard

July 19, 2016

Grateful acknowledgement is made to the following editors and publishers in whose publications (including online) earlier or final versions of some of these poems and reminiscences first appeared: *Seasonings of the Milky Way, Blue Moon & Literary Art Review, Dreaming Rivers Dreaming, Naked Lemons and Watermelons, Fugue, Pebble Lake Review, Artemis, Poetry New Zealand, Blue Hen Quarterly of Haiku and Zen Poetry.*

In addition, grateful acknowledgment is made to my wife, Rita, for her helpful support, suggestions, and also pictures of the author in each of these volumes.

Table of Contents

Fog

A way of finding yourself
lost where fog clings. Veins of
remembered playlight begin to blur.

Steady heart, wave battalions
pound and blast. You cannot see
them, only savor a restlessness
that whomps as April's blood.

Who you are erases here like a native
earth present in unseen praise.
Masks of rock jut out beyond
the sea and sadness.

Like the you
you once thought you were
they appear to accept this orchestration,
a reminder that fogscapes
are the mind's deadly poem, those
questioning streets
borne in difference.

Old Skins

Sunflowers once spotted
with blood, blossom as cinderellas
in summer thunderstorms.

Once seen as a moon,
the onion
breaks form and peels
off skins of a former self.

Sometimes in pools
of sunlight
time is detailed
by a multitude of eyes,
the fashion or hue
of cargos, gowns of garlic,
the sperm of ganders
and the pink iris
of a heart that never rests.

Darby and Joan

In this wild summer
as sunflower blossoms
flicker in the breeze,
Darby and Joan
enjoy English muffins,
chicken broth, and Tivoli beer
by the French doors
of the Seahorse Bar and Grill.

They are crazy about
shin-embracing waves,
the rush of terns and Herring gulls,
and the sea blue rustle of pines
next to sand spits of sperm
and sandwich wrappers.

They listen to
the coppersmith's hammer
and the shucks of oyster farmers.

In this global village
of gay young men and pregnant girls,
thunder clashes
of rider cymbals,
smells of leather
and unearthed dreams,
a father and daughter fly a kite
called "gold star in the red west."

2

As a chorus of shadows
deepen on the grass,
cello and bassoon
music flows over them
by fields radiant with joy.

Endgame

I see that inner fire
That makes angels of dried bones
In deserts where you ride this stallion
Across miles and miles of naked soul.

I hear your love slow down and die
In those unresolved confessions
Dying into death's sudden song
And still in some way you resurrect
All that weaves us as earth.

I watch the love you call love
Become winters of familiar fits
And wear out in drifts of unnatural light
Our tomorrows try to feverishly forget.
You try in every love to find
Love that is blind, in front, below, divine.

The love you love vanishes
Demands those remains of you
You cannot unearth to share.
So you replay the search, the craving, the dying
For the love that empties with every love.

Castor and Pollux

In trees of the wood
we notice a floating
maple leaf as maples
spill down summer's page

while river barges
merge with
traffic of the tides.

Widening circles
include the ambling rivers
across Australia
and the beaches
of Long Island.

In greening meadows,
we nudge syllables
the size of molecules,
savor strawberry jam
and suck in sea fog
on the morning sand
even as death
dines on unwilling dust.

Yet we still rejoice
in common threads
and keep yearning
as far as breath can yearn.

In the meantime,
Castor and Pollux flex
their own protective fire
in the Gemini constellation
as a full moon rises
behind the pine and fir trees.

Sailor Years

While pulling up chickweed
and shepherd's purse
in our backyard,
I notice standing corn
ripening
near a field of stags and hares.

I think of my sailor years
sailing through
the not-so-obvious
and remember how
Odysseus soon realized
he and his crew must move on
for there is a transition
from natural man,
that is, a lotus-eater
and his unremembered ages,
to being a surviving hero.

He must have known hell,
history, and heaven
are also within us
beneath a circling sun
and forests
with unnumbered leaves.

By the garden wall,
I also notice
the horse chestnut trees
and woodwinds
of the sky
where poetry and music
seem to kiss
in their own alphabets
of meanings
and interplays of earth light.

Full Circle

In this wide galaxy
with its strings
of uncharted galaxies
and splintered lights,
we know nirvana
explodes literal truth
and that history
may be abolished.

In the meantime,
we swim the river at midnight,
pluck grass by the handfuls,
hoist sails to the winds,
shape wood for fences,
drum limericks,
and through thickets of briars
note the crescent moon,
foothills that oxidize silver,
and outlaws who resume
their time circles in the dark.

In pleasing our appetites
we often come full circle.

Monte Rio Bridge
(Wedding Anniversary, Highland
Dell Lodge, August 11, 2014)

This a.m. fog clings
to the tree tops.
A slight breeze
licks its tongue
across the currents
of the Russian River.
After a breakfast
of bacon, eggs, toast,
orange juice, coffee
we stroll to the balcony.
No one is at the beach.

In the lobby, we read the
New York Times,
the *San Francisco Chronicle,*
and the *Russian River Times.*

This afternoon, as we stop
on the bridge and gaze
at the beauty of the fir,
pine, and cypress trees,

6

we watch as the sun invites
families to the beach
with their red, green, and yellow
air mattresses, beach balls,
inner tubes, water guns,
and beach chairs.

There is a low river level
due to the drought. A little
girl walks all the way
across the river and the
water only gets up to her waist.
A father squirts his son
and daughter
on their air mattresses
with a long orange pump squirt gun.
They splash him back.
Some mothers gab
while watching their kids.
It is a sunny day about 88 degrees.
More families unload their cars
and station wagons.
Despite the drought,
the river lures them
as it does every summer.

Stolen Kisses

In wartime
many want
to live in peace.

Sooner or later
stolen kisses venture
beyond the warzones
and barrier reef
as lithe summer winds
wave over dappled waters.

Once the fog lifts,
daylight crackles
through the Norway maples
and Monterey pines
throughout our lovesome years
as we translate
pulsations into
grapes of wine light
beyond our fields
of contemplation
to where combines leave
rakes of threshed hay
bony with light.

Hemispheres Ago

Once hoarfrost disappears,
and bronze green hills are warmed
by golden red sunlight,
wild geese honk overhead
as I fish for verbs
in days of bread and work
to sketch it all.

Just as music strums
the earthy strings of feeling
in this land
of classically sculptured corn fields
and grass green forests,
cows with bulging udders
are in the barn
once the farmer
is done in the fields.

What was din and grief
keen hemispheres ago,
we now voyage
toward cabalistic tomorrows
as we enjoy Damson plums

and cream cheese
on blueberry bagels.

Yankee Clipper

The view from our canary-colored hills
to the moss green sea
is a kind of music
worthy of bards
with tongues of forked lightning,
soliloquies of
wind and water,
as summer's tide
spills onto the beach.

We are surprised
to see a Yankee clipper,
an anachronism,
cruising the cliff-bordered
fjords of our shores.

Meanwhile, his farm work
completed and
with a sunburned face
our ranch hand, Luis,
corrals a palomino and buckskin
as starlings gyrate
and swoop
above our vineyards.

True Name

After a breakfast
of French toast, eggs Benedict,
and Kona coffee,
we use guided imagery
in a search for your true name.

As a shawl of fog
stitched with morning mist
lifts along the shore,
you visualize
the timeless strokes
of oracular archives
as well as nymphs
from blue grottoes
seeming green
in meadows
by the sea-blue sea
with its briny fragrances,
coral shells, and
waves pulverized on the rocks.

You also visualize
the crackling white blaze
of a sensual summer
awash with shearwater birds.

In a final reckoning,
we find
that moon, sun, and sea
are your true name.

Ozzie and Alanna

At dawn's piccolopasso knees,
an old-fashioned hipster
and maiden
with golden-red hair
watch a sorrel filly
canter by
as though in a succession
of tawny-boned summers
and mulatto sand dunes.

Theirs is an amorous story
the color of waves
full of surf and spume

as they enjoy meat,
Evian water,
and new potatoes
at the Roadhouse Café.

They listen
to a viola da gamba
and acoustic bass guitar
play jazz.
(Nothing beats live music.)

They also cherish
each drop of sunlight
and the psalm-like contours
of this tongue of summer
with the scent of a rose.

Passages

Come death or come dawn,
slicing time
happens in visible drops.

You may be
in your sleeping clothes
between forks
and the moon,
workshops of
the sleeping naked,
or vessels loaded
with geometry.

Between the tumble
of errant waves
and geological cathedrals,
you can become fond
of maritime stanzas
and the thrums
of green guitars.

There is a
dashing radiance
in the eyes of a starry night.

There are always
in the waters of now
liars, thieves, and autumn
truth-tellers in silent husks
of an undressed wind.

Breakable Bodies

Though we live on Grub Street
as senna trees blossom yellow,
we still have
our fig leaf ice cream
smooth as a pearled abalone shell.

As my first cousin once removed,
we know love's secret lines
since what makes a poem
is the history embraced,
especially the unspoken
history between us.

Season after seasoned
migrations of the phoenix overhead,
you have learned to be gentle
as wild peaches bowl their harvest
down our path
in this unhurried river valley
with its music of untold turnings,
where butterflies whirl
in the long sunlight,
and late-night fishermen
listen to every stroke and blossom.

Anatomy Show

After wandering an entire night,
I behold women
who cast frail shadows
dancing through streets
carpeted with flowers
like waves
on a glassy sea.

In the blue hues
of an autumn evening,
it was another anatomy show
where they teach
muscles to think
in another way.

They drift by
like a blue blossom
that has taken light years
just to be here.

Freight

Much to carry: silks, Muslim
dances in the rawhide sun,
perfumes, rose bushes,
Venetian red tables, mangoes,
horseshoe crabs, sponges,
Norway maples, moccasin flowers,
grapes, bananas, beef tongues,
aluminum, New York ferns,
tiger's eyes, gaffer's tape,
mandolas, whistle flutes,
and apple green jewels.

The crew does its jobs and
when not on watch eat pot-au-feu.
Some laugh and joke at the southern sea

which invites a broken knowledge
that soon resurrects
memories at each port of call.

All these are there when the ship docks,
bringing life to a solitude of books
and the dance of miracles.

Running Bear

Though she had her choice among princes,
she knew we weave the web given to us
even though,
as waves billow against the hull,
the past is a receding shoreline.

She found that
among tenants of the heart,
they quickened each other
as they ran
with the morning wind
in cloaks of pale mist.

They seemed to always find
a moment seasoned for thoughts of love
as they gazed afar
to locate a favorable fortune.

Our original perception
is not always the last one.

Summer Swallows

Not the fug of a deserted shack
but the poseidon sea's zesty winds
and aroma teeming with tuna,
squid, whales, sharks, lobsters, and lingcod.

Instead, early summer swallows,
endless plumb line tunings,
mulatto wheat fields,
vertical lines of an eland,
spark the ensign colors
of such unspoken offerings.

No, this rapunzel summer
offers a view
to form
gold strands with syllables
of fear and kinky play
as well as
the wordless subtlety
of a Vermeer radiant dawn.

A Country Churchyard

Below a cloudy Mount St. Helena,
we stroll among the gravestones
of a country churchyard
and wonder how folks got here.

Most are probably parishioners
who lived as farmers, shopkeepers,
cattlemen, and even clergy
as well as some who spun their days
in rural idleness.

They all had to deal
with time's tricks,
the ambiguous piss of borders,
and maybe some sensed
tomorrow would not be
like it used to be.

We reach a road
that stretches far
among the spruce and oak trees
and begin to walk

along the star jasmine
that borders it.

Cobblestones disappear
in the underbrush.

None of this stanches
our minds in ash-blonde motion.

At one point,
with arched brows,
we find a rhinestone brooch
that still glitters.

Amazing what you may
discover in a country place.

Twilight Bathing the Trees

How I remember you
in Oaxaca, Rio, Macao,
Prague, New York
standing next to
Segal's *Gay Liberation*
with a black beauty salute.

Even your nudity
at the beach,
incited unspoken offerings
in the amorous tendencies
of the flesh
to make
another's summer green.

You sublime troubadour
with a wild heart,
so dedicated
to your science
among the living,
sketching shadows

of an albino moonlight
in the final ringing
of a lonely graveyard bell.

How I remember you
in Winnipeg,
Aix-en-Provence
at the Musée Granet
or sketching
water shadows on long walks.
You always gave that knowing smile
when you heard
the humming of bumble bees,
saw a wedge
of Canada geese in "V" formation,
breathed the honey dashes
of summer,
studied Olmec jade art
in the shimmering plenty,
or were enchanted
by a buffet
of the moon at dawn,
moving mountains,
and twilight bathing the trees.

Yes, I remember you.

Color Music

Silence is its own color music:
what's blue
in a man's blue moments
is not blue forever;
always there is
the cast of green memory
as the moon rises
over ivory sands
and African masks
by a river

17

near another river
that bleeds larks in the night
at a pinpoint in the future.

Rivers of the Sea

I watch the ducks and the fishermen too
And the woman who threads by the water.
A dog's tied to the rail of the trailer
She bought way back when her clothes were brand new.
Somehow she survives though not like who's who
In a rich loneliness but through hangers
Loaded with skirts and pants and choice strangers
Along the way. Beer, bread, potatoes, stew —
These bones help firm her blood. The fishermen
Too wait at low tide, their poles pointed straight
Down the river's 3/4 time. They chat low
In pink sails of the wind as a gull tends
The reeds. And the ducks? They mate and await
Greener currents, sometimes yes, sometimes no.

Backstreet Poets

Charmed by the fragrance
of a green flower
as we listen to Borodin's
On the Steppes of Central Asia
and some funky music
beneath this blood moon
after a harvest inside a dream,
we have trekked
through narrow nights
in rugged mountains
in the company
of backstreet poets, comrades,
and journalists.

Black and white verses

careen from heavenly inspiration,
sermons of rivers,
and starry regions in heaven's heart.

Fishing

In a world with a banged beginning
beneath sunset-red cirrus clouds
waist deep in the damp
of this low island,
one fish leaps and ripples
this lake by a forest of fir and pine.

The fish dwell
in a berg of sunken seasons.
I could stay here forever
despite the dung
of low-flying geese and mallards.

Nostalgia cloaks me when I come here.
I hate the sense of leaving
for death is more than ashes.

Should we be so lucky and intelligent,
maybe this earth can outlive
our greed and ignorance.

Beneath a Purple Sky

a church aspires with its spires
reaching heavenward toward

other intelligent life in our infinite
universes and billions of galaxies away.

As the bells of its belfry toll softly, the sacred heart
looks inward to unite with the human faces of God.

Just another day beneath a purple sky.

Quitting Arms

It seems that for every advance
into graciousness and kindness,
it is the spring of another war-monger
who likes his wine
the color of blood and agony.

Still there are also
those whose love
lasts through
the magic
of each epoch and
echoes of the beating heart of silence.

Their love can be
drum skin tight
over the passing years
without an angry word between them.

In the twilight of their eyes,
last words of love
can be music and poems
for those who sleep
as wild winds blow on sandy dunes.

Transubstantiation in Blue

yes as lovers we flow
to the sounding sea
poundings the sea hallows
the ever sun-brided sea
you rising out of the me
of me you pine for
in the sunshivering sea
the elements you pine for
in the sea of me

we lovers school the sea
flushed with rebirth
communing loins like
plucked ganders of foam
you can rise from the illusion
of me like mendicants burning
to deep kiss the holy noon

we lovers go to
the resounding sea
in a schooner of souls
herdings past history's
fume and rack
and again you rise
out of the sea of me
with no illusions
of fireless voices
or the politics of hollow eyes

we lovers school the sea
in threshed enskyment
in madness and sad guitars
in summits of unshouldered beauty
in drums of brokered eyelids
connoisseurs of sunslips and slapsilver
we lovers school the sea

Sweet Milk — a System of Signs

A woman dressed in treble clefs
dreams of love
becomes a gate for angels in designer genes.

She translates the sign
"Blue at the bottom of the pool"
and smiles as though armed with a smudge of suns.

She muses how everything certain
is hidden
in the swishes of a solitary falcon's wings.

Still she dreams, sings to the moon
dancing in the lake.

Her song points to a tranquil night's passage,
a swing of beauty's sign
restored to an icon called time.

First Fish

Circular to the last, you can retrieve the first.
Imagine lips parted as though to resort to chemistry

As you troll a virgin river without end.
The lines at first seem endless. Then other tests
At twenty, fifty, and eighty, each stress
accents a new catch on another's line.

Matters soon taste all-too-human, assume
A visible diction—bass, pike, sunfish—shades of an
ancient name.

Imperceptibly it becomes harder to snag that first one.
You can retrieve simplicity, the way your first hook,
Hallowed by the everyday, is struck with new luster.

Imagine trolling the river of those departed.
How tunnels at both ends light, hook of that eye
first opening.

Embracing Metaphors

Unclear jellyfish in the reeds I am,
That mighty zero, primal astronomy.
Your disappearing fact, an atlas in stages,
A phrase within a phase, my blue fountain:

This collection of cravings, one last kiss,
An extended family in ecstatic prayer.
I'm in transition, a ghost perky in levitation,
A melody within a malady.

Swanhilda

In a capful of sea wind
beneath an ultramarine sky,
I drink my pearl tea.

Using my deceased wife's binoculars,
I can see islands that seem
to rock with my newest love's return.

Meantime, I watch breakers
foam the shore
by a meadow
sweet with hay
near a foxtail pine,
blackberry vines,
and apple blossoms.

Though styles and fashions
zip by, I still love to listen
to the beat of her genius
and enjoy the
rainbows of her dark irises.

The Land of You

I know how much
you love porter beer
like Newcastle Brown Ale
and comfort food
like mashed potatoes
and gravy,
corn on the cob,
and hot apple pie.

You have them
even in your garden
of late parties
with the sights
and sounds of fireflies.

23

We both know land
to be an encyclopedia
of light and shadows,
yoga breathing,
and nomads
as grizzlies snooze
in southern Yukon.

Land is more
than ribs of earth
and eyes
of the four winds
from Mexico City
to Herat,
Johannesburg,
and Flamengo Beach.

As you drink
your sweet, hot,
and blond coffee,
trees leaf
to a rainbow
of green, amber,
vermilion, and orchid.

You have a secret
fondness for sunlight
between storms
by hills hemmed in by mist.

blue jays filled with sunlight

silent now
the peace of lilies

Or Not To Be

Imagine my headstone
in a joyful churchyard;
barely can you scrape the moss
with your fingers to see my name
and dates in this particular galaxy
and even the word "poet" beneath it.

Or my ashes in a small corner of
a garden by a pool, now in spirit,
now in free love, with ice age
companions of sunshine, rain, snow
and thaws with rice, roses, blackberries,
rainbow colors, and the speaking
silence of the divine.

Muirfinn

In the bagpipes of memory,
his kilt
umbrellas out
in the quarter-notes
of every day
as he drifts between
the land of Nod
and dreams
in which the trappings
of clowns include
dictions of the thumb.

And then there's awakening
to the gentle rocking
of a catamaran in our cove,
not to mention
the underfoot echoes
of passing trucks and limos.

25

Meanwhile, the sky
festers with crows and sparrows.

Soon he puts away his canvas,
brushes and easel
and, as night dawns,
begins his sleepwalking
tour of our cove.

Horoscope

You check your horoscope:
"Neptune sliding out of *Pisces*
takes your delusions
of forgetfulness with it."

Most around us
hear your raffish laughter
in this cornflower blue summer.

You love bonfires
at the beach
as tour buses line
the resort parking lot.

As your fictive kin,
I am part of your family
of different ages
counting up
whether it is among
the electric hums of crickets,
caverns in a mountain side
dotted with susurrant oaks,
or beneath flights
of migrating cranes
and monarch butterflies.

We know art,
even as a mirage,
defies brevity

in a stelliferous sky
or green isles
bunched with lilies
glorious as Solomon
silent among old stones
warmed by the western sun.

Such are some sacramental visions
of a wide-arched grace.

Diago

As this postilion canters
his appaloosa above the sea,
he notes pelican-gray waters
peopled with images
in this diocese of gulls.

Here and there,
ropes of kelp sway and turn
in this instant
that is paradise.

Sea winds awaken
in his hair
and there is a sea smell
on his shoulders.

In the higgledy-piggledy
music of this seaside
net of waves,
time simply disappears
in mazy murmurings
as surfers hunt beachcomers
so they can put on rainbows
as flavors of the day.

His appaloosa tugs
on the bridle
and is ready to continue,
this time walking

but not as fast
as a Tennessee Walking Horse.

Close Encounters

Fortune smiles
as the star of morning rises.

The sun wheels around
ancient forests
and the weight
of island foam
as we have
another close encounter
with our homeland's
household voices.

In this grape autumn,
two converging brooks
make our meadows green
as birds wing landward
from a roiling sea.

We sit down
with our club sandwiches
and Evian water
and note the shifting currents,
wind flowers, and sandy breezes.

Soon fireflies
show us
their shadows and splendor
through the maples leafing out.

Feather Tree

Once we place
the Hackle-Flue Feather Tree
next to the lyrics

of little bo peep
and have some fresh-brewed coffee,
we venture out
in the ormolu slants
of sunlight
at our summer place.

Footprints jogged
down the beach
is a rich resort
for the bummed-out
and restless
peopled with
the common nationality
of pigmentation
and unwhispered dialects.

We mark a barrier beach
and see how sea weed and sea
drench the strokes of time
as azure stone falls
from a summer of good fortune.

In glorious proofs of revolution,
we pass an enclave
of lavender-loving lions,
a labial heart
of the pear tree,
and doves with
a waist of twittering leaves.

Purple Haze

In spite of harsh wrinkles
of deep sorrow,
having survived
in a purple haze
terror's velvet fist
and time's tempestuous sea,
he still notes stars

in a trout's eyes
and in utterless thought
unearths a thread
of infinity
in the skin
of each body's voice.

He rejects
the selfishness that mocks
the inward span
of a man
as taxis and vegetable trucks
pass by.

At the Keggersdude Café,
he orders
a pasta puttanesca
and a Grgich Hills Chardonnay
as a red moon rises at
the amber edge of sky.

Whispers Throb

In the moral mindscape
of a primaeval forest,
a land of promise,
where whispers throb
with vision and desire
in the old tongue,
there occurs
a sea-green vision
of a sacramental earth.

In the refracted light
of a unforgiving summer sun,
there are
dawnlit roots
smelling of rosemary
or on the beach
where a godlike sheen emerges

as unconscious waves replace
the fealty of memory,
flowers, with their susurration leaves,
bloom in their own time
as a cargo of diamonds
arrives at a navy dockyard.

Random Reminiscences

October 31, 1953. When I was 8 years old, my sister Lani, a couple of neighbors, and I went trick or treating on a dark Halloween night with just a small flashlight and the light of a candle inside a pumpkin. On a dark road in the country there were very few lights. Soon I spotted what looked like a snake in the road about 20-30 yards ahead. I asked her what we should do. She said "let's keep going and we'll see what happens." I was really scared but we kept going and it turned out to be simply a piece of rope. Boy, I was so relieved! There could've been more snakes for all I knew. But I looked up to her for advice and leadership and I never forgot that evening.

April 1959. Went with Allen Brune, Hiram Feldman, and Dave Brune to Hunt's Dam. We had to make sure the gate was closed since that meant no one was on the property. Sometimes when we went and the gate was open, there was a caretaker in a 1953 gray dodge coop who came to Hunt's to keep an eye on the property. This time the gate was closed; over the gate we went. We were simply going to take a swim and have a good time. The only fish in the reservoir were minnows and other small fish. I remember Allen run and take a shallow dive in the water now made brown since his dive stirred up mud from the bottom. This time we had a mud fight and getting mud all over us, we now had a reason to dive in and wash our bodies off. Our swim and mud fight over, we sat for awhile in the gentle breezes that passed through the pine and oak trees. The cabin, used by the Hunt family when they visited, was locked tighter than a drum. In time, this reservoir, named

31

Lake Lu-El, would become my Walden Pond and high school class mates such as John Hazen and Bob Eggers would come up there with me. It was a fun time.

June 10, 1971. Ketchum, Idaho, 1971. Hemingway house. drove to the "no trespassing" sign. Strolled in. Wild yellow flowers cover the hillside leading to the redwood house overlooking the Big Wood River. Asked the white-haired gardener if I could come up to the balcony. He said yes. His name was Benny. A native of Pamplona, Spain. Came over to this country with Hemingway. He was delighted to hear I had been to Spain, including Madrid and Barcelona. We talked and talked. Less than fifty yards away, the Big Wood River rushed and gurgled along.

Then went to the Hemingway Memorial in Sun Valley three miles away. About fifty yards off the road is a memorial with a bust of Hemingway and a quote from him apparently composed in 1939.

June 21, 1971. Took a leisurely stroll up Camp's Road just prior to the fall of darkness. What stillness! Sheer delight. Moths hover around the perennial oaks while sheep paused to stare as I passed as if I was a good shepherd. The stars came in like theatrical lights: some suddenly, others gradually. The dome of heaven is on fire with love. Black Angus steers grazed contentedly, their bells tinkling in the distance. A jay screeched from a top of a tall evergreen. Its screech ruptured an otherwise almost completely silent night. My footsteps were the most immediate sound. The Doppler Effect. What crickets could even hear me long after I had left that part of me yards behind? How brief is even your sounds. Amazement and wonder: the twins of letting be, a witness to happening. Splurting hoses from irrigation pipes also rent the evening. Smells of fresh-cut hay circulated and the lights we make to be eyes of night, the protectors of unguarded moments, optic nerves that compete with the stars as man's extension, burned through oak and elm. The stillness brought silence in her train. Something curious about stillness and silence. They make you take a double take. The first take is to say: Why? The second is: Wow. There is something that is articulated only in private moments, in silence. The way the sun casts its shadow at dusk or twilight. It reminds me of John Donne's "Good Friday 1613, Riding Westward." You see that shadow, the way the light hits, divulges a certain hue, silent tones of the wind. It is the arrow of eternity and it pierces the heart. Maybe it is the slant, touch, and unreasoned bone that are a fleeting moment, a dashing intuition of the permanence who remains unrevealed.

July 29, 1971. Rode toward the end of Foster Road at sunset. Hay covers the hills and dry weeds crackle with gusts of the wind. Vineyards look lush in the distance; there is a wide westerly bend in the Napa River that slowly flows with the hills as backdrop. Eucalyptus Lane exudes its usual charm. Nature is the place of the divine: building, factories are all artificial. Technology, business are urban phenomena; most are urbanized. Perhaps that is why we thrive on artificiality.

August 6, 1971. This evening a full moon lights the dying sky; each dog, horse, cow watches with an intense alertness, readied for a moment's bark, gallop or ringing of the cow bell. The horses neigh and toss their manes. A spotted hunting hound pierces the night with his extended bark; the cows are content to graze. The night breathes its throaty song through the parch-dried hay-colored fields and hills. The wind is always a source of a thousand images in the creative mind. The Ensele family the other night was playing hide-and-seek. They have two Shetland ponies and a large palamino grazing on their two acre lot.

August 9, 1971. Rose at 4:15 this morning and drove to my friend Jim Herrman's house in Rohnert Park. Both Carol and Jim were up. Had a cup of coffee before we left to fish at Bodega Bay. Went through the lush heavily-forested Russian River country. We ate a quick breakfast mom had fixed for us. The brownies were delicious. We shot the breeze with two old foggies who were, as it turned out, were jackasses. One boasted how many deer he had killed in Utah and Colorado; the other bragged how he had shot a 2,100 pound elk (1,465 pounds dressed). That is braggarts for you! Then, after hearing more bullshit, we decided to drive out to a long stretch of land owned by the U.S. Coast Guard culminating in a series of rocks from which we fished at low tide. Herm caught a large, long smelt that fought like a hell's angel on a charge of chastity. He caught another one later; our bait (squid) did not do the trick. It brought no fish; caught a ½ pound yelloweye rockfish on shrimp.

At 3:00 or so we decided (or rather the wind decided for us like the Greek fleet for Agamemnon) to leave. The winds were at least 30 m.p.h. We returned to the Tides wharf restaurant. Herm drank beer; I, a Coke. We gazed at the girls in short shorts. The small fishing fleet docked at the wharf. Then we gazed at the fresh salmon in the bait shop, disappointed because we had not caught any fish half so large. Content with our catch (somewhat), we ventured home, eating red licorice most of the way.

September 18, 1973. My brother Carl came to Nashville today. I showed him the Vanderbilt campus, including Furman and Kirkland Halls and the Divinity School and its library. Then on to Belmont College where I am teaching philosophy of religion this semester. Then we went to the U.S. District Court House to hear his lawyer friend named Barrett argue a case. Next day, after Carl slept on the floor of my little apartment, they were off to a conference at Sea Island, Georgia.

November 25, 1973. Met Joseph Campbell, the historian of religions, emeritus at Sarah Lawrence College, tonight just before his Vanderbilt lecture on the psychologically deep myths and symbols and their meaning for us in the technological age. Warm, witty, charming, erudite, Campbell has the speaker's gift. A delightful man. I told him his recitation of Wordsworth's "Tintern Abbey" the night before was a delight. I told him I was a student of Suzuki, Alan Watts, and Heinrich Zimmer. At the reception following in the Tillett Lounge, we discussed Alan Watts' recent death. His funeral was done by Buddhist monks; one monk took a candle and flame and waved it, saying "Alan. Go!" Campbell and his wife lit incense to commemorate Watts' passing. We also discussed the permanence of symbols of dying and resurrection and why the western tradition places a primacy on the discursive intellect. Campbell was a sheer delight, a man who has, I believe, attained bodhi.

October 14, 1974. New England in October. An Oktoberfest. Picture postcard days, falling leaves, windswirls of falls long past, Civil War cannon, chills of New Hampshire lakes, farewells all through Indian summers, harkenings of pumpkins, cornstalks and quaint wooden bridges, tastes of apple, white rocking chairs reflect the bright, clear sunlight chilly in sweaters gladly pulled on in cold mornings warmed by heavy blankets. Seasonal rhythm, temperature drops. Gentle rises of Vermont's hills, kaleidoscopic colors of fall in New England. Harvard playing Yale, of Bowdoin, of Dartmouth: colors cue the season. A poem of changing earths, a tapestry of traditions, enlarging us with seasonal awe.

March 1, 1975. Left Nashville at 9 a.m. en route to Philadelphia. Went north to "Bowling Green, Kentucky then east to Glascow. Stopped at the Dairy Queen for a cup of hot coffee; read sports page of Louisville-Courier Journal. Found radio time for Vandy-Kentucky basketball game. Headed east again to Columbia then Campbellsville then Harrodsville. Saw Shakertown briefly; filmed a description of it on a plaque by the highway. Saw Asbury Theological Seminary, a small conservative campus. Onto Lexington as I listened to the basketball game in which Vandy lost 108-84. It was snowing on the little ponds, lakes, and farms and fields in Kentucky. Tractor and hay-trucks sat idle as snowflakes pelted the windshield. Cattle chewed their cud, ignoring the snowflakes.

Ashland, Kentucky: a small mining town on the river; the smell of smelters and ore mines was overwhelming. They seemed to strangle everything. Pollution everywhere. Soon crossed the bridge over the Ohio River into Huntington, West Virginia. No motels around so I continued driving. Finally came to a motel: Stone Lodge Motel $14.40 a night. Too a hot, luxurious bath after driving four hundred miles. Afterwards I ate a pork sandwich and chef salad at the Stone Lodge Restaurant. Then I retired on a full stomach and freshly-bathed body. A fitting end to hours on the road.

March 2, 1975. I left Huntington, Charleston, Ripley, Spencer, Glenville, Weston, Clarksburg, Grafton, then into Maryland, Oakland, Maryland which was in the middle of a snowstorm with a temperature of 17 above zero, visibility was almost nothing. Tried to head east, bound for Cumberland, Maryland but the hills were too slippery. The car began to slide flip, flop. Finding I could no longer proceed toward Cumberland, I turned around and headed for western Pennsylvania. Crossed the state border around 8 p.m. Stopped at Laurel Highlands Motel, eight miles east of Uniontown, Pa. It is run by Evelyn Fabinoff, a medium sized woman of dark complexion and dark brown hair. She was quite distrustful and asked for $9.54 in cash. Fortunately I had the cash on me. Got my bags into the room, turned on the TV and took a hot bath. Then with Mannix (a TV detective) on, I am writing this journal entry about to study Chinese and translate Chinese sentences. It has been a harrowing day and I regret trying to drive the Comet in the mountains.

March 3, 1975. Arrived in Plymouth Meeting, a suburb of Philadelphia. I had already called Professor Charles Fu from Morgantown at 4:15 p.m. He said to call after 6:00. Arrived and got a room at the George Washington Lodge, a high-class motel for a starving student at $20.00 per night. Then called Dr. Fu again. He gave me directions to his house. Finally found his house. He met me at the door. He is short with fairly short hair, wears large black glasses, very insistent in his manner. Very enthusiastic about Heidegger, Zen, and Taoism. Volumes in Japanese and Chinese fill his shelves. He teaches Buddhist, Taoist, and Zen thought and is trained in the western tradition of philosophical analysis at the University of Illinois. He is very much publishing minded but a creative thinker. Nervously smokes long filter-tipped cigarettes. A good sense of humor, a serious scholar and has all the low-allowed emotion traditionally seen in the eyes of Asians precisely because they *are that* emotional. We talked of Tao, Heidegger, Zen, analytic philosophy; he would like me to come to Temple University. He wrote a letter to the chairman, Paul Van Buren, recommending financial aid.

We had some cherry wine. He kept trying to get me to drink whiskey. But, being a Methodist, I only drink wine, beer, gin and rum. And, when in Japan, saké.

March 4, 1975. This morning left George Washington Lodge. Went to Vince's Gulf Station and had right rear wheel looked at. It was in bad shape, but he said it would simply go out but had many more miles left on it. So I drove to Chestnut Hill train station, parked the car, bought a ticket, and got on the train for Temple Station. In about twenty minutes, after about a dozen stops, arrived at Temple, a mass of concrete, unimpressive buildings. Talked to Paul van Buren, a death of God theologian; it is a dubious vocation at best tinctured with a philosophical naiveté. I gave him Fu's letter. He said he did not know the financial situation and was thus not very helpful.

Then I attended Dr. Fu's seminary on Mahayana Buddhism. A focus was the problem of identity in Chang's book on Hua Yen philosophy and Heidegger's book *Identity and Difference.* Met Mr. Lee, a Korean, a Mr. Chang, a man named Darrel on sabbatical from Muhlenberg College, Steve Heine, a cool guy from Temple; Tony Zylenkas who gave a report on Heidegger; Ellen Delmore, an intellectual student from Kansas City, Mo. with long ivory fingers and charity-chaliced blue eyes who is thirty-two years old. Some nice looking women but Philadelphia (or any huge city) just doesn't do it for me. Nashville is an exception: some might think it is big, but it remains small. I left on the train, remaining ambivalent about coming to Temple since I had also been admitted to the graduate program in East-West philosophy at the University of Hawaii.

Tonight, I called my classy uncle, the lifelong Marine and Mississippi State alumnus, Beverly P. Veal. He said to come on down to Virginia. He had served in World War II, the Korean War, and two tours of duty in Vietnam.

March 5, 1975. It is only fifty-six miles to Maryland from Philadelphia. I soon missed the correct turn and was off in Rising Sun, Md. Drove a re-route to Elkton, Md. Along Susquehanna River, the river where Southey and Coleridge wanted to establish their utopia in America. Finally reached a route that would connect with Highway 13 in Blackbird, Md. That would take me to Salisbury, only 128 miles from Philly. Drove through Delaware with its flat country of two-story homes and miles of farm land and small towns. Seven miles south of the Delaware border is Salisbury, a small town known for its fishing and transportation industries. Stopped at a BP station, got gas, and called my paternal great uncle, Dr. Seth Hunter Hurdle, M.D. He said to come on by. He is a graduate of the University of Virginia medical school in 1920. Later, he became public health officer for Wicomico County and earned a master's degree in public health from Johns Hopkins University. (A public health center is named after him in Salisbury). He lives at 423 Somerset, not far from Salisbury State College. He is about 6'1" tall, a large man, bald on top, with brown eyes and the manner and wit closely resembling my late father, Thornton C. Bunch. He said to me: if you are as half as smart as your dad, you are very smart. I replied: I am probably at least half as smart. He must have been referring to my father teaching college chemistry as only a sophomore at New Mexico School of Mines in Socorro, New Mexico.

His wife, Elinor, is white-haired, arthritic (especially in the hand joints), and has that characteristic of ongoing comparison of statuses that is a trademark of women in the family. This elevated everyone and oneself in the process. Across the street their daughter, Patti (a Virginia nursing school graduate), lives with her husband, Chris Mitchell, M.D. (another Virginia medical school graduate). Seth, Sally, Elizabeth, Hunter(?). Bobby Phillips, another daughter and her husband "Fuzzy", and their son, Bob and _____(?).

We had manicotti made by "Liz," a senior nursing student at the University of Richmond. We talked the night through.

March 6, 1975. This morning had right rear ball bearing repaired at a Texaco Station. I went to a nursing home with Dr. Chris Mitchell. We started off the day with a prayer breakfast. I met all kinds of businessmen and other professionals. A generally good experience was had by all.

After lunch at a restaurant, I left Salisbury bound for Portsmouth, Va. Arrived around 5 p.m. Saw Brian Veal (later a chiropractor in Atlanta) and his friends, then Beverly, and finally Audrey. Their daughter, Penny, was away at school. Went into their home and had a nice dinner. Watched TV and talked late into the night.

March 7, 1975. This morning we visited Trinity Episcopal Church cemetery; saw the graves of my ancestors Thomas and George Veale, who were on the vestry in 1762 and were members of the First Families of Virginia. We also visited Oak Grove Cemetery where my maternal grandfather, David Almer Veal (1878-1948) who married Laura Rose Pennington of Raleigh, NC; Almer Judson Veal (1913-1920), a victim of the Influenza Epidemic of 1918, and Kimberly Shearin Veal are buried. Then we drove over to Monumental Methodist Church where the Veals are members. I met their minister Dabney Walters, a bald fellow with much charm. It is the same church Bishop William McKendree served from 1790-1792. That night I saw the ACC semifinals: North Carolina beat Clemson. It has been a full day of activities. Delicious steak.

Saturday, March 8, 1975. This morning around 11 a.m., Bev, Audrey, Brian and I left for Colonial Williamsburg. We drove across the Jamestown Bridge over Nansemond River to Newport News. Around noon we arrived in Williamsburg. We visited the College of William and Mary (1693) where my mother was to go; instead she married my dad. We strolled around the Christopher Wren building, the oldest college building in the U.S

(1695), which is well-preserved. He is the famous English architect and scientist whose masterpiece is St. Paul's Cathedral in London. Then we walked to Bruton Parish Church (1715) which is done in typical colonial style with high walls between the pews and ornate choir loft and elaborate pulpit. Churchyard outside full of graves including a Galt, one of my distant relatives I think. Our family on the Veal side is related to the Boling and Galt families of Virginia. Then we went on to the Governor's mansion with its long lawn up to it. We did not go in the mansion. Then we strolled past restaurants with lines of people outside. We did not want to wait in a line that long. Saw the silversmith and gunpowder shops but did not linger.

We left and drove to Jamestown Island, site of the first permanent English settlement in the New World (1607) after several attempts to found colonies in North Carolina in the 1580s. I saw a statue of Pocahontas, (my ancestor), John Smith and the ruins of the first church in Jamestown.

Then we went on to Yorktown where Lord Cornwallis surrendered the British army to the combined American and French forces in 1781, thus ending the American Revolution. In Yorktown, we ate at a Greek restaurant called Nick's. I had a seafood plate; Bev had crab; Audrey and Brian had shrimp.

Then we returned to Portsmouth. That evening, Bev and I went to my great aunt's house. Mrs. Sallie Baker, 83 and Ivan Baker, a Syracuse man, who is 87. They are a devout Baptist couple. I took pictures. Met Sallie's daughter, Mary Nell (Baker) Roosendaal and her husband Al. After an hour or so, we bid them farewell. Really liked Sallie (Hurdle) Baker. She is my great aunt, grandma Nell (Hurdle) Bunch's sister.

March 9. Left this morning for Nashville.

March 30, 1976. A springtime in Pennsylvania. The wind cuts through Germantown in March like a scythe. Summer comes hard. Spring is birth pangs. I still like going to Leaves of Grass bookstore on my way to taking the subway to Temple University at Broad and Montgomery.

Spring is birth pangs. Winter begins to loosen its grip and knows it must relinquish to the sweet air and blooming flowers of spring. How roughly its hates to give up its four or five month hold. Ice thaws. Flowers thrust their heads into the growing sunny days.

Fog is beautiful as well. It covers all and gives a mask of unreality to trees, sky, and humans. A cool 52 degrees outside.

October 14, 1974. New England in October. An Oktoberfest. Picture postcard days, falling leaves, wind-swirls of falls long past, Civil War cannon, chills of New Hampshire lakes, farewells all through Indian summers, harkenings of pumpkins, cornstalks and quaint wooden bridges, tastes of apple, white rocking chairs reflect the bright, clear sunlight chilly in sweaters gladly pulled on in cold mornings warmed by heavy blankets. Seasonal rhythm, temperature drops. Gentle rises of Vermont's hills, kaleidoscopic colors of fall in New England. Harvard playing Yale, of Bowdoin, of Dartmouth: colors cue the season. A poem of changing earths, a tapestry of traditions, enlarging us with seasonal awe.

March 1, 1975. Left Nashville at 9 a.m. en route to Philadelphia. Went north to "Bowling Green, Kentucky then east to Glascow. Stopped at the Dairy Queen for a cup of hot coffee; read sports page of Louisville-Courier Journal. Found radio time for Vandy-Kentucky basketball game. Headed east again to Columbia then Campbellsville then Harrodsville. Saw Shakertown briefly; filmed a description of it on a plaque by the highway. Saw Asbury Theological Seminary, a small conservative campus. Onto Lexington as I listened to the basketball game in which Vandy lost 108-84. It was snowing on the little ponds, lakes, and farms and fields in Kentucky. Tractor and hay-trucks sat idle as snowflakes pelted the windshield. Cattle chewed their cud, ignoring the snowflakes.

Ashland, Kentucky: a small mining town on the river; the smell of smelters and ore mines was overwhelming. They seemed to strangle everything. Pollution every-where. Soon crossed the bridge over the Ohio River into

Huntington, West Virginia. No motels around so I continued driving. Finally came to a motel: Stone Lodge Motel
$14.40 a night. Too a hot, luxurious bath after driving four
hundred miles. Afterwards I ate a pork sandwich and
chef salad at the Stone Lodge Restaurant. Then I retired
on a full stomach and freshly-bathed body. A fitting end
to hours on the road.

March 2, 1975. I left Huntington, Charleston, Ripley,
Spencer, Glenville, Weston, Clarksburg, Grafton, then
into Maryland, Oakland, Maryland which was in the
middle of a snowstorm with a temperature of 17 above
zero, visibility was almost nothing. Tried to head east,
bound for Cumberland, Maryland but the hills were too
slippery. The car began to slide flip, flop. Finding I could
no longer proceed toward Cumberland, I turned around
and headed for western Pennsylvania. Crossed the state
border around 8 p.m. Stopped at Laurel Highlands Motel,
eight miles east of Uniontown, Pa. It is run by Evelyn
Fabinoff, a medium sized woman of dark complexion
and dark brown hair. She was quite distrustful and asked
for $9.54 in cash. Fortunately I had the cash on me. Got
my bags into the room, turned on the TV and took a hot
bath. Then with Mannix (a TV detective) on, I am writing
this journal entry about to study Chinese and translate
Chinese sentences. It has been a harrowing day and I
regret trying to drive the Comet in the mountains.

March 3, 1975. Arrived in Plymouth Meeting, a suburb of
Philadelphia. I had already called Professor Charles Fu
from Morgantown at 4:15 p.m. He said to call after 6:00.
Arrived and got a room at the George Washington Lodge,
a high-class motel for a starving student at $20.00 per
night. Then called Dr. Fu again. He gave me directions
to his house. Finally found his house. He met me at the
door. He is short with fairly short hair, wears large black
glasses, very insistent in his manner. Very enthusiastic
about Heidegger, Zen, and Taoism. Volumes in Japanese
and Chinese fill his shelves. He teaches Buddhist, Taoist,
and Zen thought and is trained in the western tradition
of philosophical analysis at the University of Illinois.

He is very much publishing minded but a creative thinker. Nervously smokes long filter-tipped cigarettes. A good sense of humor, a serious scholar and has all the low-allowed emotion traditionally seen in the eyes of Asians precisely because they *are that* emotional. We talked of Tao, Heidegger, Zen, analytic philosophy; he would like me to come to Temple University. He wrote a letter to the chairman, Paul Van Buren, recommending financial aid.

We had some cherry wine. He kept trying to get me to drink whiskey. But, being a Methodist, I only drink wine, beer, gin and rum. And, when in Japan, saké.

March 4, 1975. This morning left George Washington Lodge. Went to Vince's Gulf Station and had right rear wheel looked at. It was in bad shape, but he said it would simply go out but had many more miles left on it. So I drove to Chestnut Hill train station, parked the car, bought a ticket, and got on the train for Temple Station. In about twenty minutes, after about a dozen stops, arrived at Temple, a mass of concrete, unimpressive buildings. Talked to Paul van Buren, a death of God theologian; it is a dubious vocation at best tinctured with a philosophical naiveté. I gave him Fu's letter. He said he did not know the financial situation and was thus not very helpful.

Then I attended Dr. Fu's seminary on Mahayana Buddhism. A focus was the problem of identity in Chang's book on Hua Yen philosophy and Heidegger's book *Identity and Difference*. Met Mr. Lee, a Korean, a Mr. Chang, a man named Darrel on sabbatical from Muhlenberg College, Steve Heine, a cool guy from Temple; Tony Zylenkas who gave a report on Heidegger; Ellen Delmore, an intellectual student from Kansas City, Mo. with long ivory fingers and charity-chaliced blue eyes who is thirty-two years old. Some nice looking women but Philadelphia (or any huge city) just doesn't do it for me. Nashville is an exception: some might think it is big, but it remains small. I left on the train, remaining ambivalent about coming to Temple since I had also been admitted to the graduate program in East-West philosophy at the University of Hawaii.

Tonight, I called my classy uncle, the lifelong Marine and Mississippi State alumnus, Beverly P. Veal. He said to come on down to Virginia. He had served in World War II, the Korean War, and two tours of duty in Vietnam.

March 5, 1975. It is only fifty-six miles to Maryland from Philadelphia. I soon missed the correct turn and was off in Rising Sun, Md. Drove a re-route to Elkton, Md. Along Susquehanna River, the river where Southey and Coleridge wanted to establish their utopia in America. Finally reached a route that would connect with Highway 13 in Blackbird, Md. That would take me to Salisbury, only 128 miles from Philly. Drove through Delaware with its flat country of two-story homes and miles of farm land and small towns. Seven miles south of the Delaware border is Salisbury, a small town known for its fishing and transportation industries. Stopped at a BP station, got gas, and called my paternal great uncle, Dr. Seth Hunter Hurdle, M.D. He said to come on by. He is a graduate of the University of Virginia medical school in 1920. Later, he became public health officer for Wicomico County and earned a master's degree in public health from Johns Hopkins University. (A public health center is named after him in Salisbury). He lives at 423 Somerset, not far from Salisbury State College. He is about 6'1" tall, a large man, bald on top, with brown eyes and the manner and wit closely resembling my late father, Thornton C. Bunch. He said to me: if you are as half as smart as your dad, you are very smart. I replied: I am probably at least half as smart. He must have been referring to my father teaching college chemistry as only a sophomore at New Mexico School of Mines in Socorro, New Mexico.

His wife, Elinor, is white-haired, arthritic (especially in the hand joints), and has that characteristic of ongoing comparison of statuses that is a trademark of women in the family. This elevated everyone and oneself in the process. Across the street their daughter, Patti (a Virginia nursing school graduate), lives with her husband, Chris

Mitchell, M.D. (another Virginia medical school graduate). Seth, Sally, Elizabeth, Hunter(?). Bobby Phillips, another daughter and her husband "Fuzzy", and their son, Bob and _____(?).

We had manicotti made by "Liz," a senior nursing student at the University of Richmond. We talked the night through.

March 6, 1975. This morning had right rear ball bearing repaired at a Texaco Station. I went to a nursing home with Dr. Chris Mitchell. We started off the day with a prayer breakfast. I met all kinds of businessmen and other professionals. A generally good experience was had by all.

After lunch at a restaurant, I left Salisbury bound for Portsmouth, Va. Arrived around 5 p.m. Saw Brian Veal (later a chiropractor in Atlanta) and his friends, then Beverly, and finally Audrey. Their daughter, Penny, was away at school. Went into their home and had a nice dinner. Watched TV and talked late into the night.

March 7, 1975. This morning we visited Trinity Episcopal Church cemetery; saw the graves of my ancestors Thomas and George Veale, who were on the vestry in 1762 and were members of the First Families of Virginia. We also visited Oak Grove Cemetery where my maternal grandfather, David Almer Veal (1878-1948) who married Laura Rose Pennington of Raleigh, NC; Almer Judson Veal (1913-1920), a victim of the Influenza Epidemic of 1918, and Kimberly Shearin Veal are buried. Then we drove over to Monumental Methodist Church where the Veals are members. I met their minister Dabney Walters, a bald fellow with much charm. It is the same church Bishop William McKendree served from 1790-1792. That night I saw the ACC semifinals: North Carolina beat Clemson. It has been a full day of activities. Delicious steak.

Saturday, March 8, 1975. This morning around 11 a.m., Bev, Audrey, Brian and I left for Colonial Williamsburg. We drove across the Jamestown Bridge over Nansemond River to Newport News. Around noon we arrived in

Williamsburg. We visited the College of William and Mary (1693) where my mother was to go; instead she married my dad. We strolled around the Christopher Wren building, the oldest college building in the U.S (1695), which is well-preserved. He is the famous English architect and scientist whose masterpiece is St. Paul's Cathedral in London. Then we walked to Bruton Parish Church (1715) which is done in typical colonial style with high walls between the pews and ornate choir loft and elaborate pulpit. Churchyard outside full of graves including a Galt, one of my distant relatives I think. Our family on the Veal side is related to the Boling and Galt families of Virginia. Then we went on to the Governor's mansion with its long lawn up to it. We did not go in the mansion. Then we strolled past restaurants with lines of people outside. We did not want to wait in a line that long. Saw the silversmith and gunpowder shops but did not linger.

We left and drove to Jamestown Island, site of the first permanent English settlement in the New World (1607) after several attempts to found colonies in North Carolina in the 1580s. I saw a statue of Pocahontas, (my ancestor), John Smith and the ruins of the first church in Jamestown.

Then we went on to Yorktown where Lord Cornwallis surrendered the British army to the combined American and French forces in 1781, thus ending the American Revolution. In Yorktown, we ate at a Greek restaurant called Nick's. I had a seafood plate; Bev had crab; Audrey and Brian had shrimp.

Then we returned to Portsmouth. That evening, Bev and I went to my great aunt's house. Mrs. Sallie Baker, 83 and Ivan Baker, a Syracuse man, who is 87. They are a devout Baptist couple. I took pictures. Met Sallie's daughter, Mary Nell (Baker) Roosendaal and her husband Al. After an hour or so, we bid them farewell. Really liked Sallie (Hurdle) Baker. She is my great aunt, grandma Nell (Hurdle) Bunch's sister.

March 9. Left this morning for Nashville.

July 29-30, 1978. This weekend I went canoeing with two other law students, Mark Harris and Roy Chamlee, at the Eleven Point River in Missouri. It was a fun, but tiring time. We slept in a tent. Sounds of locusts pierced the night air. During our trip, we saw three or four water snakes. Add to that, our canoe capsized four times since we are such experts at canoeing. We had steak for dinner over an easily-built fire at Whites Creek Camp about five hours paddle down toward Riverton, the place where we disembarked.

The next morning, we discovered we forgot our bread. It had been left in Roy's car. We ate breakfast nevertheless. I cooked half a dozen eggs; we drank milk and ate knifefuls of peanut butter—ugh! Before leaving around 10:30, we explored a cave about a quarter mile from our campsite. It was sticky on the entrance floor. We all wore sneakers. It was eerie; two or three bats darted our way but missed us.

We left and paddled down river. Roy and I in one canoe; Mark in the other. It cost us $38.50 for two canoes for two days. I was over-exposed to the sun and as a result had a helluva headache thanks to not eating right and also felt nauseated. We drank a case of beer, Busch and Strohs, between us.

I enjoyed getting to know my fellow law students. Roy's dad teaches at Belmont College and Mark studied both psychology and theology at Emory University in Atlanta. We had some good discussions. Over the next year or so, Roy and I would enjoy many Pink Panther movies while eating popcorn. Also, it was also enjoyable to go out to Mark's place in Germantown for Halloween Hayrides and apple cider. It was a rather delightful break from studies just like Phi Delta Phi rush parties were.

September 19, 1980. Left this morning at 4 a.m. with Richard Desaussure, a fellow Circuit Court law clerk, and head to Arkansas to take highway 57 north to Cairo, Illinois. Known to CB radio listeners as "Leprechaun," Richard traced the smokeys (highway patrol) throughout the trip. We stopped for gas in Missouri and ate at

Sambo's just south of the Illinois line. I had an omelet, pancakes, and coffee; he had English muffins and coffee. We drove to Rantoul, Illinois where we had lunch at a Dairy Queen: good ole fast foods. It was hot, the corn was short due to the heat wave of the summer of 1980, and the flatness of central Illinois made driving boring but easy.

We passed the turn-off to the University of Illinois at Urbana-Champaign. Arriving at the turn-off to South Bend, we drove bumper-to-bumper around Chicago; we soon took an off-ramp and hit another route that allowed us to circumvent the traffic jam. Soon, rising above the trees off to the south was Notre Dame's Golden Dome, the home of the Fighting Irish. We arrived on campus around 4:00, that is 12 hours on the road.

After meeting Richard's friend, Andy, we went to the engineering building since Richard majored in civil engineering at Notre Dame. He graduated in 1977. We talked to Dean Marley, currently assistant dean, and then strolled across campus to the bookstore where a frenzy was building up for the next day's game against the Wolverines of Michigan. Sweat shirts and jackets were being compared and tried on by eager Notre Dame fans. After buying a pennant and a history of Notre Dame football, we went to Andy's place, the Castle Point apartments.

After relaxing awhile, took a shower, and got ready to visit Father Sorin's prodigy, Notre Dame. We had a sausage and pepperoni pizza at Rocco's — it was fair. Then Richard and I went to the Notre Dame pep rally, a sweat box to the tune of the repeated lyrics to the Notre Dame fight song. After thirty minutes of blood-curdling, spirit-building noise, I had to go outside for some fresh air.

Then we toured the campus library, Rockne Memorial, dorms, etc. Later we returned after unsuccessfully trying to get into the senior bar.

September 20, 1980. We were awakened by the bright light from the drapeless windows of the Castle Point apartments. Took a shower and then we all headed to the campus. Saw the various campus clubs selling freshly-cooked hot dogs, steaks, hamburgers; stands with Notre Dame buttons, pennants of Stanford, Michigan, Notre Dame line the walkways hawking their wares. Thirty minutes before kickoff, we saw the Notre Dame band begin to march to the field. Visited the Athletic Convocation Center with all the Notre Dame trophies: national champs, Cotton Bowl, etc. Saw the game ball from the 1925 Rose Bowl between Knute Rockne and the Four Horsemen (Crowley, Stuhldreher, Miller, and Layden) against Pop Warner and fullback Ernie Nevers (from Santa Rosa). Final score: Notre Dame 27, Stanford 10. Would love to have seen that game, especially since I went to Stanford.

Since it was already sprinkling while we drank Harp Beer, imported from Ireland, at the Senior Bar, we decided not to try to secure tickets. Instead, Richard bought Stroh's and I bought Hamms beer and we watched the local telecast of the game. Notre Dame beat Michigan 29-27 by a field goal on the final play of the game. It was truly a thrilling finish.

Bought a N.D. stat book and a short-sleeve shirt at the N.D. bookstore. Some cute girls were on campus.

After the game, we ate at a steak house, then returned to the apartment.

September 21, 1980. We got up early, said goodbye to Andy, took some pictures of the campus; then headed south.

We had breakfast at the Golden Bear Restaurant: Richard had a "Papa Bear Special." I had a pizza omelet. We managed to avoid the smokeys, including "2 county Mounties" and "2 full grown bears" all the way through Illinois with Richard's CB radio. It was a fun trip, a chance to be with a fun friend and to see a football game at South Bend, a real treat.

June 19, 1981. Richard and I were introduced to the Tennessee Supreme Court in Nashville by our senior partner Harold Horne in the Memphis law firm of Horne and Peppel before Justices Harbison (chief justice), Brock, Fones, Drowota, and Cooper. After we were sworn in, we had lunch at the Laughing Man Restaurant, a vegetarian delight: steamed veggies with a Pink Cloud (strawberries, milk, bananas, and honey). Then we took a tour of another alma mater, Vanderbilt University, home of the Commodores.

March 4, 1982. I cannot forget the poetic pathways that, like paths through the woods, lead me home to tranquil lakesides such as Hunt's Dam in California. Sunny spring days beside the lake, reading Emerson and Thoreau, are fond memories. At times I forget that every human heart is human. In the push and pull of businesses, we lose track and forget much that is well to remember. At times I am so caught up, I have to get out those mystic, thoreauean woods and remember my moments at Walden Pond. Hunt's Dam is my Walden Pond. I cherish every sound of the bullfrogs and crickets and quarter-moon over the redwood bridge with the words "Tiger Dam" written on it. I call it Hunt's Dam since it belongs to a Mr. Hunt. How fresh the grasses look on a spring morning with sunslants penetrating the dew-laden grass. That makes me want to paint. Then those stagnant pools thick with algae, a biologist's paradise: single-celled organisms, especially paramecia, under the looking glass. There are truly so many wonders in this world, opened to us by the precision-based hands of science that the mystery of it all begins at best to touch the wonder that is God. The emotional inspiration of the design argument: Whitman: "O farther, farther sail!/ Are they not all the seas of God." For me, religion and science flow hand in hand.

August 18, 1983. Took a twilight walk up Buhman Avenue. Oaks beckon you to climb their moss-decorated trunks and limbs. The hay-colored hills, the silver-streaked skies, the cows grazing on the hillsides, the perfect climate for grape-growing, poetry and philosophy. Echoes of that Keatsian line apply to Napa Valley hills: "Thou unravished bride of quietness..." I love the silence of the woods. My spirit is refreshed. I become more deeply aware and grandeur-inspired in the face of Beauty.

November 7, 1983. I said goodbye to a relationship that was not working out. The pain, excruciating in moments comes with it. But time eases the pain. Trust time to undermine the heartache. Tomorrow will be a brighter day. Another love will swim into your ken. Despite the hurt of a broken relationship, you live to learn to love again, and again, and again. Such are the natural rhythms of life.

March 30, 1984. I took a part-time job at the Best Western Napa Valley Lodge, in Yountville. It sucks. The nicest part is the drive through the lovely valley in which I grew up. Yountville is quiet, conservative, and quaint. It caters to the tourist trade that has blossomed for the valley whose wine is, as Robert Louis Stevenson said, "bottled poetry."

May 13, 1984. I went to my 20th high school reunion. Talk about the tooth of time, how some classmates have mellowed, others emerged from relative obscurity, how some have lost and won. Lines of age etched in faces at mid-life. High school days seem so remote, lost in mist.

August 14, 1984. Last night I went to my sister's house. Her girls watched Call to Glory, a premier of a weekly series concerning the time (1962) of the Cuban missile crisis. Lani was working on schedules for fall; Barry was cleaning his den. They will vacation in Hawaii next week and I will house sit for them. I drank a Lowenbrau and stayed about forty-five minutes. I left around ten o'clock and viewed the sky under a canopy of stars.

September 15, 1984. I went horseback trail riding with several others on the Jack London ranch. Two hours of dusty trails, panoramic views of this magnificent eucalyptus grove, oak, wild blackberry vines, dry creeks, hay-covered clearings. There is also London's algae-covered, bird-enclaved lake, and narrow, stony creek-side paths. It was therapeutic. Fir, pine, redwood dominated vistas lush green to the western hills, rolling vineyards glistening leaves in the late afternoon sun. Jack would be proud. Valley of the Moon is exquisite.

November 3, 1984. Today I hiked on Jack London's ranch up to about six miles above the reservoir. Hiked through an apple orchard, lovely oak leaf beds, pine trees and pine needle beds; saw two faun that bounded into the enclaves of oak beyond the hay-colored clearings that periodically appear on the trail. Now I am reading London's *Martin Eden* which is atypical of the London stereotype as merely a writer of tales of the sea and of the Yukon.

March 19, 1985. The old house, 1251 Foster Road, currently owned by Art Duff, has deteriorated — no lawn mowed in backyard, no fish pond. It is grotesque to return to places that have changed, in this case, a part of me that is lost forever and dimmed by memories. I walked up Foster Road, past the old Grossi place where I played cowboys and Indians in the second grade, turned up Hilton Avenue, then Grandview Drive. At Camp's Ranch, saw many sheep grazing in the lush fields. Occasionally a mother sheep would tilt her head at me, and then return to her grazing.

Then I walked down old Camp's road where it has not been used in a long time as shown by the thick berry bushes that had spread out across the road. A couple of horses grazed contentedly on the hillside. I viewed the house from the rear; it had deteriorated. What a job my father did; the place was in tip top shape when he was alive. The place is worlds away from that time.

March 20, 1985. I was a substitute teacher today at Irene M. Snow Elementary School in Napa for Mrs. Borders, another poetry lover. After school was out, took another nostalgia trip. This time I walked up Hilton Avenue to my Walden Pond, Hunt's Dam. I went in the open gate, far enough so I could see the wind whistling on the waters. Then I saw an old man and a dog at the gate. There I was trespassing again. It was Mr. Munger and his dog. He gave me this neighborhood information: Mr. Hunt died around 1980 the lovely cabin of my dreams was inherited by his nephew who now resides here with his wife and baby. Apparently he works in Walnut Creek.

My own version of Walden Pond is now occupied. For years no body lived there from the time it was constructed in 1955.

Also, next to the Hunt place and presumably a part of it, was sold to another relative, who made his money in the clothing business named Wailes, plans to use that part of land to sink $750,000 into a luxury mansion and breed Morgan draft horses in a beautiful stable built for housing them. Munger was full of neighborhood gossip. I love it!

After awhile I left, got in my car at Snow, and drove home.

May 5, 1985. Visited Herm and family today. Chinese food, Carol's 38th birthday, cake, ice cream. Herm is a friend of 30 years this fall. Friendship is one of the true gifts. Cherish it.

August 27, 1985. Fishing at Kentwood Lake in Marin County with Herm. No luck. Then we went to the Jack London Ranch and hiked to the reservoir. Time flies. Noticed it in the aging on Herm's face. Mine is a mirror. Both of us are 40 now. I'm still living life and working my tail off. It has been a hectic summer. Girlfriend left (another bird of appetite?) I wrote for the *Napa Valley Times* as a journalist and associate editor. Also I taught American History at Napa Valley College and sat for the Bar again in Sacramento. I am exhausted!

October 5, 1985. Left for Jack London ranch at 1:30. Had just called my friend Jim Herrman to go fishing next weekend; told him I was going to the Jack London ranch. He invited me to drop by for dinner. I said I would. Told me his mother had had a stroke about two weeks ago. I was sorry to hear about it. He said it was serious.

Arrived at the ranch around 2:30, about 25 miles from Napa. Paid $2 admission. Visited again Charmian London's "Happy Walls," the house dedicated to Jack, build in 1919.

Hiked to the reservoir on the ranch. There were about six or seven people. I listened to the radio. Flies began to irritate me. It was in the 80s or 90s and the heat felt concentrated.

Around 4:30, I hiked down the hill, past the pig palace, cement silos, and the cottage where Jack wrote. Down to the cement driveway. Checked my radiator since it was leaking. Watched some riders on their walking horses pass by me.

Arrived at Jack London bookstore around 4:50 and began to browse. Many of London's books can be found there that one cannot find anywhere else.

Found a copy of *The Star Rover* which was published by an occult-astrology publishing house in Malibu. Looked for a collection of short stories called *On the Makaloa Mat*. When I read Russ Kingman's biography last year, he mentioned these works, written late in Jack's life. Jack had been reading about Jungian psychoanalysis and other totally different themes.

Looked at *The Star Rover* with its astral body projections and reincarnation. What a shift from tales of the Yukon and the South Seas, and themes of the wolf. It is as if London had made peace with the astrological, spiritual heritage of his parents, Flora and "Professor" Chaney. He was searching for newer themes, newer earths, and newer seas.

I began talking with Winnifred "Winnie" Kingman about when *Makaloa Mat* would be reprinted and she said the copyright would be in the public domain in about ten years. During the conversation, I inquired into the descendants of Jack and whether any of them had literary interests. She said Joan London had written a book. Becky London who lived in an apartment next to the bookstore, but mostly loved writing letters. The family was not very ambitious and had not inherited much drive from Jack.

Winnie went into the adjacent room. In a moment a white-haired woman emerged. I was introduced to Jack's daughter, Becky London who graciously talked with me. Since she was hard of hearing and wore hearing aids, I had to talk much louder than I normally would have.

She was about five feet six inches tall, large framed and talkative. I asked her some questions about her dad:

How tall was Jack? About 5'7" or 5'8."

How much did Jack weigh? 165 pounds. Later, when he was suffering from uremic poisoning due to kidney malfunction, and taking bella donna, morphine, and heroin to kill the pain, he was up to 180 pounds. He died at age 40 probably due to overdoses of morphine.

How old were you when your father died? Fourteen.

What are some of your best memories of your father? He would select books from the library and put them in a basket. She would then read them. Also, she knew Jack, not as a world-famous author, but simply as "Daddy." She said she saw her father as rarely as once a year. From 1907-1909, he was on the voyage of the "Snark," a boat he built. And during the last couple of years of his life, he lived a good part of the year in Hawaii. She was encouraged to write her father and did so.

I asked her what films her father was in. She said he was in the filming of *The Seawolf* and also a short flick taken five days before he died, which is at the ranch itself. It is a push button affair at Happy Walls, showing Jack in his wagon and later holding squirming piglets from the pig palace on the ranch.

Becky is almost 83, loves baseball with the Oakland A's, San Francisco Giants, and the San Francisco 49ers football team. She autographed a copy of Jack's *Seawolf.* It reads: "for Richard Bunch, it was so nice talking with you about Daddy. He was a sailor among other things. Sincerely, Becky London, October 15, 1985, Glen Ellen, California."

It was nearly six o'clock when I left for Herm's house. What a delightful experience it had been to meet the youngest daughter of Jack London! I was on Cloud Nine! For many, such an experience would not mean much. But for a person who has been writing for twenty-one years, it was paradise.

Such spontaneous events are, to me, the kaleidoscopic possibilities that occur and are spice to an otherwise prosaic day. Welcome events like that. They make life bounce with renewed vigor and meaning.

October 12, 1985. Went fishing at Lake Berryessa with Herm today. Got two bites. One guy and his wife caught a 14" trout with help from his net. A warm, autumn day located just up the road from the U.S. Reclamation office. Fished from 9:00 to12:45 then went to the Turtle Rock Café. Each of us had a hamburger and a beer. We watched the customers: the Chinese bartender smoking his cigar; the tall, skinny cowboy-hat wearing patron who took the $3.50 I paid for the minnows we used. Some Mexican teens played pool sporting newly-sprouted mustaches. A middle-aged woman in a blue sweater cooked our burgers and brought them to us at the bar. There is a large aquarium at one end of the bar. Swimming around leisurely were a large turtle, a small bass, and assorted smaller fish. Among the many signs and slogans in this bar-café was one that indicated the unique flavor of this place. It reads: "Have a nice day — asshole." With encouragement such as this, you should make your reservations early. It was, shall we say, interesting.

After leaving the café, we drove to Napa in Herm's grey VW station wagon to visit his mom who was in Queen of the Valley Hospital. It had been years since I had seen Herm's older sister, Val, who has a warm smile. She was there, also waiting for the notary to notarize powers of attorney so that they could pay his mom's medical bills as they came due. The notary himself was recently a patient in the intensive care unit. Forever it seemed he took to notarize the general and special powers. Hard of hearing, he practically yelled at Herm's mom who was not fond of having everyone congregate around her bed. Doubtless, he wanted to make sure she heard him but his voice could summon the dead. Nearly thirty minutes later, everything was done. The twenty dollar bill had been paid and later Herm drove me home. We talked awhile and agreed to attend the Jack London Festival at the Jack London State park the next day.

November 5, 1985. Appointed to the Housing Authority/ Building Authority Board for the City of Napa and will report primarily financial transactions to the Board of Supervisors and be sworn in by Napa's Mayor, Harold Solomon.

May 10, 1986. Today I went to Hammerhorn Lake in Mendocino County with Herm and his son, Chris. We left at 8:30 and stopped for breakfast at 10:30 at McDonald's in Willits. I had a "big breakfast" (such a poetic name): eggs, English muffin, and a sausage patty and a large coffee. Both Herm and Christopher had Egg McMuffins.

Then we gassed up and traveled north to Dos Rio and on to the little country town of Covalo which was filled with "dudes" wearing cowboy hats. Many "dudes" were gathered at Covalo's main hamburger place called the "Burger Station." We went into the general store since Herm wanted to top off the gas tank. Inside, there were Indian blankets for sale on the counter; they averaged $28 and were hand-made by the local Indians on the nearby reservation. Crowds were on every street corner. We inquired what was going on. The lady in the general store told us it was "field day" in Covalo. I walked next door and picked up a copy of the *Round Valley News* newspaper. It was thin, mostly ads and a few TV programs.

Leaving Covalo, we went past city limits and turned right and drove about ten miles before we turned left on Hammerhorn Camp Road. For the next twenty miles, it was dirt and dust on the road leading into Hammerhorn Lake. The road is usually closed in winter due to a mountain slide a couple of years earlier. The slide had filled in ½ of a small lake far below. Onward and upward we plodded, dust clouds trailing us. After an hour of traveling between 15 and 20 mph, we finally arrived at little campground that sits on a hill. The lake is about 75-100 yards away, depending on where you set up camp. Around 1:30 we took our fishing gear to the lake and began to fish. The lake stretches 250 yards long and is only 85 yards wide. Its deepest part appears to be on the north side—at most 15-20 feet. By 3:30 I had caught ten rainbow trout; Chris ten; and Herm eleven.

Shasta sandwiches (a bright yellow marshmallow and a red salmon egg) were the special on the menu. No matter how many times I tried, the lures I brought did not work even in a favorable setting like this.

Chris' luck with lures was better. He caught most of his fish on lures, the most effective being the rooster tail.

To the camp we returned where we filleted the trout and delighted our palettes with rice, trout fillets and ice cold beer. The sky was pearl blue, the redwoods whispered as though an ocean roar, and we all sat by the fire. Herm's friend, Dave Brown and his wife, Lori, joined us.

It had been a beautiful, warm but chilly day. We were happy and contented as we watched the sun set. At dusk I hiked around the lake and observed the lily pads in the center.

Our tent slept about four persons. It took about twenty minutes to erect. Temperatures dipped into the 30s that night; I froze. I slept in my parka, bulky knit sweater, levis; and shoes on—and still froze.

Daybreak: I rose about 6 a.m. Herm got up to go to the john. I asked him to build a fire. He said he would. Christopher was sound asleep with the sleeping bag up over his head. I could not believe anyone could sleep on a night this cold. Never have I liked cold weather. And it was cold! The only other times I had been as cold was: once in Stratford, England when the coin-operated heater went off since we (Gar Davis and I) ran out of money and the December chill froze us to the bone; the other time was when I was a student at Temple University in Philadelphia: twice during the winter of 1976 the apartment house ran out of fuel oil. There was consequently no heat; I kept warm at 3:30 a.m. by the gas stove burners until the fuel oil truck arrived at 6:30 a.m.

To return to Hammerhorn Lake: once Herm's fire was crackling, I got up. No need to put on clothes since I had slept in them. As I emerged from our tent, the briskness of the cold morning air slapped my face. Quickly I headed for the crackling flames and stood there, thawing my front side, especially my hands. It had been 8 or 9 hours since I had felt half way warm.

Herm's gas stove was on; I began to cook bacon. One burner was nearly empty and only warmed water. Our first cup of coffee was warm. We then put some tin foil over the water pot to keep the heat in and the next few cups were much hotter. The bacon cooked slowly; its aroma was delicious. It made cooking outdoors a delight. Hot coffee over an open fire and the aroma of slowly-cooked bacon made camping and fishing an outdoorsman's dream.

Although the slow-cooking bacon made my mouth water, I was still stuffed from the trout fillets of the night before. I fixed bacon and eggs for breakfast; Herm kept the fire going and washed dishes once breakfast was over.

We then decided to walk to the lake to fish; the sun was over the tall redwoods on the eastern side of the lake. Chris was already fishing and had caught two trout on lures. As he reeled in, the fish would follow the lure then back off as they swam too close to shore. On the northern side, still in the shadows, Herm and I saw a plethora of fish since we were high up on the bank. We called for Chris to try here. He decided not to.

September 27, 1986. Herm, Carol, and I scaled the heights of Bald Mountain in Sonoma County. An hour and a half of thigh-straining and knee-fatiguing ascent gets you on eye level with clouds that stretch long into the horizon. Views of St. Helena, Rutherford, Napa, Oakmont, Santa Rosa, Oakland, and San Francisco are among the treats for the weary. Wind and silence are hymns beneath this skyey cathedral, a vast survey for the isolato, lungs invigorated. A sense of power (views for miles) and sheer insignificance (awe at the power of the mountain). Of the two, insignificance has the upper hand. Perhaps the pinnacle of power at any level results in the realization of our own significant insignificance.

Descent was by another route; we arrived at the car by 5:30. I fixed tacos for Herm and his family. It was a peaceful night.

June 28, 1986. Today I sunbathed at Ridgeview out on the practice field surrounded by the track on which I used to compete and on the field where I used to practice when I played for Ridgeview Jr. High. The school is no longer a junior high (1955-1983) but an updated middle school called Harvest River. I have many fond memories of Ridgeview: the Fair Day booths, the sports (football, basketball, track, softball I played there), the teenage pranks and romances, and how they seemed so important at the time. It was a time when just growing from year to year seemed an insurmountable task. Just being a teenager was traumatic and exciting enough. It was when all life seemed an endless ocean, as far as the eye can see, and lay before us. Memories turn down the lamp and allow us to savor a past filtered through the matrixes of nostalgia and distance.

November 11, 1986. With Herm I went to a Sonoma State vs. Humboldt State football game. Sonoma State won 24-17, a come from behind victory. Stanford beat UCLA in L.A. to go to 7-2 on the season. Watched SSU vs. San Francisco State soccer match then went to Herm's house in Kenwood and had lingcod for dinner. It was a fun evening with French Columbard wine. I am exhausted! What with school at Sonoma State, substitute teaching, and teaching Philosophy in Literature at Chapman College, it is a hectic autumn.

May 15, 1987. I took a day off from substitute teaching and arrived at Herm's house around 10 a.m. It had been a stressful time for Hermand especially his wife, Carol, since she had been giving daily care to his mother, Dorothy, who died on May 6.

Many things were packed in Herm's station: tackle boxes, fishing poles, sleeping bags, firewood, a Coleman lantern and propane gas stove, a tent, and much food.

We left around 10:30: Herm, I, Christopher, his friend, Josh Newman and Herm's daughter, Rebecca.

On the way to Hammerhorn Lake in the El Dorado National Forest, we stopped in Willits to get beer (Stroh's Light), and pastries for breakfast. We also ate at McDonald's: a hamburger, fries, and a Pepsi.

Covalo was quiet and not much was happening. We got gas and found the long, twenty mile road freshly tarred. Arrived at camp around 4:00, nearly a six hour trip, and Dave Brown and his daughter Susan were there. They had saved us a camping spot. Since we arrived a week later than last year, campsites were crowded and fishing was less plentiful. By 5:30 the tent was up. The boys had gone fishing. I made a salad with artichoke hearts, lettuce, tomato, alfalfa sprouts, and Girard's salad dressing. It tasted scrumptious. Tartar sauce topped trout filets fished for throughout the afternoon. Cold beer washed them down. Although a cold night was expected, the nights this year were anticlimactic. At 10:30 I bid everyone goodnight and went to sleep in my goose down sleeping bag so soundly, since I had got only three hours of sleep the previous night. I did not hear the other four come to bed within half an hour. I was gone: sleep hit me quite hard.

Next morning, I was awake by 6 a.m., shaved, and had coffee with Dave Brown, a skilled fisherman, and together we went fishing. Caught four trout on Shasta Sandwiches, a yellow marshmallow and one salmon egg, which was four more than the night before. Spent the afternoon in the tent writing a report for Sonoma Sate due on Monday concerning observations in a reading class at Silverado Middle School. Fished later that evening and caught two more Rainbow trout about 9-10 inches long. The trout were smaller this year. All totaled, I caught six fish at Hammerhorn. Last year the fish were bigger and more plentiful.

For dinner that night, we had trout (what else?) and a delicious salad from the same ingredients of the night before. Susan and Josh listened to a walkman group: the Brass Monkey and the Beastie Boys. Went to bed around 10:45. My eyes closed and I soon feel asleep. Did not get up until 7:40, shaved, had some of Dave Brown's coffee, talked about his high school days in Willits when he was an outstanding guard on the Willits Wolverines football team. Later, he went to Napa College to play for the Chiefs (now the Storm) and was given a place to stay since he was a member of the team. He worked as well by driving a bus for the Napa Valley Unified School District. Since I was working on my teaching credential at Sonoma State, he thought Sebastopol would be a fine place to teach high school.

Briefly fished on this overcast morning when we were to leave. On the way back to Kenwood, we stopped and got milkshakes at the "Burger Station" in Covalo. Later, we bought lunch, a Wendy's salad, in Ukiah, only an hour or so from Santa Rosa.

Returned to Herm's house. Carol and her mom, Merle, had been and waiting for us and working on the bedroom where Dorothy had been staying in her final illness. Herm cleaned the fish and gave me five. I said goodbye and arrived back in Napa dirty and tired. Unpacked and went to sleep. It had been a pleasant fishing trip.

June 14, 1987. I went to the funeral for Herm's mother at the Episcopal Church in Pleasant Hills. Herm's sister, Val, and Val's family, including Bob, Karen, and Michael, was there. A short service was tastefully done by a woman Episcopal priest.

August 28, 1987. Yesterday spent a marvelous day beneath cloudless blue skies at Del Rio Woods Beach on the Russian River. Listened to the melody of the falls; only about a dozen people there. Lifeguard was bored stiff. I sunned for about three hours and read text *People and Our World* which I will be teaching to 9th graders at Napa High School this semester as part of student teaching requirement for a teaching credential from Sonoma State University, home of the Seawolves. It was a peaceful, relaxing, gorgeous day, the winding down of summer. Such a death deserves a lamentation of sorts.

October 4, 1987. I visited today Tor House in Carmel, the home of poet Robinson Jeffers, that brooding Old Testament prophet like Jeremiah, that Spinoza-like pantheist reborn in the loins of a son of a staunch Presbyterian Calvinism lately gone to seed.

Lover of earth, hater of civilization, Jeffers saw the encroaching Philistines line Scenic Drive with real estate parcels and homes. You cannot stop or even retard the collective ignorance of humans. Native Americans had a stake in opposing even Jeffers from moving to Carmel. In Jeffers, we have the tradition of prophets like Jeremiah and Amos without the structure of classical theism. Anthropocentric theism has been rejected; instead pantheism and a refuge in a cosmological perspective is what "saves" Jeffers from the logical end of his rejection of classical theism.

At times, his poetry is loose and akin to Faulknerian prose. No wonder he would offend self-assured poetic neo-classicists like Yvor Winters.

October 11, 1987. Yesterday in Berkeley, I saw Cal tie Arizona 23-23. I went with my bro-in-law Barry and an old high school friend, John Hazen. We bought pizza slices at *Blondies*, ate them on the lawn of the apartments on Channing, drank beer, ate nachos with garlic bread upstairs at *Kip's Burgers*, a college hangout. A fun time and a partly cloudy day.

March 9, 1988. I received today a letter informing me my poem "For All the Ducks I've Fed Before" was the second place winner of the fifth annual Artemis Poetry Contest. This contest takes place in Roanoke, Virginia. The prize was $50 and publication in Volume XI of Artemis, a project sponsored by the Friends and Artists of the Blue Ridge Mountains in Virginia. It is an honor since it is the first official recognition for my poetry. It is also the first time I have ever earned a penny for my poetry and I have been writing the stuff off and on for twenty-four years! It made my day.

April 9, 1988. A bright day. I drove to Fort Ross, one of my favorite places. Green grass lines the cliffs; no fog today. Bikini-clad women stretched on blankets. It was hard to keep my mind on haiku! Wrote ten haiku on the beach at the cove. For once, a fog bank did not engulf the fort. Views of the beach and a herd of about sixty harbor seals were spectacular. One seal ventured within thirty yards of me. Once he saw me, he dove back in. But first he twitched his whiskers back and forth much like a philosopher's delight upon detecting an example of creeping solipsism.

July 29, 1988. Visited Del Rio Woods on the Russian River. Got a sunburn after three hours. Wrote a poem of the same name. It was inspiring.

May 3, 1989. Today I picked up another biography of William Wordsworth. For some reason he continues to fascinate me. Perhaps it is because of his ability to put philosophical ideas into his nature-centered poetry. Perhaps it is because I have traveled the Lake District and viewed the lush Cumberland countryside and unspeakable beauty of the lakes or the fascination of the friendship with Coleridge. Wordsworth's description of nature still refreshes, his insights inspire. Along with Shakespeare, Keats, and Stevenson, Wordsworth continues to fascinate ever since I first read about the daffodils in "I Wandered Lonely as A Cloud." I have taught "Ode: Intimations on Immortality" in my Philosophy in Literature class at Chapman College in the fall of 1986. The lake district is a mini-paradise: if a poet cannot be inspired there, she or he is already among the living dead.

May 18, 1989. Reading a biography of Wordsworth by Hunter Davies. It seems Wordsworth went from radical politics, that is, praising the French Revolution and absorbing William Godwin's radical politics, disillusionment after the Reign of Terror and the takeover by Napoleon, to a complete reversal into a crusty conservatism, became a strict Tory and establishment man. At points, his obsequious attitude toward the landed gentry is rather nauseating.

Wordsworth's relationship with his sister, Dorothy, was unusual. Never have I come across such devotion between a sister and brother. At times, see the *Journals*, it borders on adoration, some might even say the incestuous. His marriage is strange, out of the blue, to his cousin

Mary Hutchinson, and the living arrangements are also a bit unusual, namely his wife *and* sister living with him. Did he sense her devotion going too far and marry to provide a socially-approved buffer between himself and Dorothy? This is a most unusual relationship. Can you imagine what psychoanalysis would do with this?

May 18, 1989. Last night I went to a poetry reading by William Mathews. I really like his poem "Homer's Seeing Eye Dog" which I had previously read in the *Atlantic Monthly*. The reading was held at Cody's Bookstore in Berkeley.

October 14, 1989. My poem titled "Meditation at Muir Beach" won the grand prize in the 70th Annual Ina Coolbrith Poetry Day Contest and a check for $50. Needless to say, I felt both humbled and honored.

November 9, 1991. Walked up Hilton Avenue in Napa today. Stillness, the magnet that drawsme: time stands still. It is a pastoral. In the Camp's Ranch (now Pappas' Ranch) the sheep still graze. There's a soft tinkling of sheep bells. They stop time. I have seen the scene a hundred times before. It is refreshingly deep-rooted like the poems of Tibullus, God's grandeur. So bucolic the scene holds me. I am drawn into a time-warp; it is the country of the soul. It is why I feel contemporary to the Bethlehem of the New Testament, the dialogues of Plato, or the metaphor of flowing rivers of the ancient Taoists of China.

May 14-16, 1993. Packed for Hammerhorn Lake. Left at noon. Headed for Sonoma State and then Herm's house. At SSU bookstore manager said to come back in late July and he would take some copies of *Night Blooms*. Then we drove over Bennett Valley Road to Kenwood. Herm had already packed too. We visited for awhile; Herm ate some of my wife's homemade chocolate chip cookies. So did I. Then we went out and in about thirty minutes loaded Herm's red Toyota truck. His daughter, Becky, came home from school. Her friend Jessica from Santa Rosa was going with us.

With the truck loaded, we headed for Santa Rosa, picked up Jessica, and headed down College Avenue to Highway 101. Once past the Santa Rosa traffic, which at various point was considerable, we picked up speed, heading north 170 miles into Mendocino National Forest. In Willits we stopped and ate at Taco Bell. Then on to Hammerhorn. It is about a four hour trip from Santa Rosa to Hammerhorn. You drive along the winding Eel River on Hwy. 162, the same route Herm's father used to drive a mobile x-ray unit truck in the late 1940s where he would take x-rays of the Round Valley Indians. I knew I would miss my family and did.

We arrived tonight at 9:15. Within minutes Becky and Jessica, both ninth graders at Herbert Slater Junior High in Santa Rosa, had put up their igloo tent. Meanwhile Herm and I unloaded the truck, leaned poles against a tree, and finally got our tent up. This was around 10:30. He has a new 2-handed pump to pump up the air mattress we sleep on. It used to take an hour to blow it up by mouth.

Next day Herm got up at 6:20 and used power bait to catch his limit of Rainbow trout by 8:30. By the time he returned I was just waking up. He put the fish in a plastic pan full of water to keep them fresh. We talked awhile in low tones as the girls were not up yet. After eating a Danish, we decided to go back to the lake and do some fishing. My Shasta Sandwiches were not the bait of choice so I quickly switched over to some of Herm's power bait. Herm kept catching them. Before long he had limited out again. Finally, I caught two Rainbow trout and was delighted. Back to the camp we went. Herm sat down and cleaned the fish.

The girls in the meantime had gotten up. They ate breakfast and practiced soccer kicks with their ball. They were bored and complained about the lack of excitement. They decided to walk a couple miles to sun on the rocks in the middle of a mountain stream. Herm and I took about an hour or so nap, which Becky thought was very boring of her dad to do.

Tonight for dinner we had: Rainbow trout (surprise! surprise!), rice, salad and my wife's chocolate chip cookies.

After dinner a van full of high school guys decided to camp out; one got out and peed before our eyes. We were not impressed with this impresario. But they soon calmed down and were much quieter than some of the other folks, especially a camp full of about fifty "good ole boys" with big beer bellies who were having a fish fry and hootin' and a hollerin' and looking for a good woman with a lot of meat on her. They were that kind.

I took a walk around the lake at dusk. Beauty all around: fish were jumping; snow on the mountain peaks; forests of quietude. I sat for a long time at one corner of the lake and listened to the crickets and bullfrogs. I missed my family. I thought long about my life, its apparent meanderings, a mild case of directionlessness. I went back to camp and observed the intensity of the stars. They were little lamps seemingly fixed forever without the distractions of city lights. Herm and I talked about much that evening.

Next morning Herm got up 6:42 and headed out. I got up about twenty-five minutes later and went fishing too. No luck for me this time. Herm caught three more. Back at camp, he cleaned them. Then we decided to break camp. Forty-five minutes later we were off to have lunch in Willits at McDonalds. We arrived back in Kenwood around 3:30. Said goodbye and drove off to see my family in Alameda.

January 12, 1991. Reading about Hawaii's history. The monarchy and its overthrow: His divine sovereignty David Kalakapua, the Merry King; reading his *Myths and Legends*. Writing stories about other times and places. They do not get too far away even in paradise. Saw 1st church at Kailua, first in the islands. Yale Divinity School men. Congregationalists. A New England architectural style just like in New Haven, New Bedford, Cambridge. Futuristic Calvinistic captains of industry in their descendants such as sugar cane and pineapples. Calvinism lasts a few generations then transmutes into the socio-political and economic arenas. In New England, Calvinism often leads to Unitarianism and religious pluralism. In Hawaii,

Calvinism leads to large land ownership, marriage with native Hawaiians, cultural assimilation, commerce, industry, and political leadership.

January 14, 1991. Rita and I drove to Volcano National Park where it was overcast and lightly raining. Viewed the Kilauea Caldera; see Mark Twain's comment from *Roughing It*. Saw craters with smoke pockets, steam vents, sulphur in the air (cough, cough) as heat can be felt in your shoes, rising and relieving the terribly high temperatures below. Took some pictures.

Deadline tomorrow for war in the Persian Gulf. I think we'll be in that region of the world for years to come. War is a periodic outbreak of collective insanity. Suppose they gave a war and nobody came. Wouldn't that be a refreshing chapter in human history? As it is, history simply repeats itself: different characters, contexts, excuses — same result: the folly of unnecessary human tragedy.

May 28, 1997. Love those young Bunchkins: Katie, 47" tall, at five years old; Ricky growing taller at three years old. Both are now taking a class in gymnastics. Infancy vanishes in the night. Little girl, little boy: loveable and trying your patience at the same time. I am the luckiest man in the world with Rita, my soul mate, and Rickykins and Katiekins.

July 25-27, 1997. Today Herm came over and we left for his son, Jimmy's house in Pollack Pines. We arrived from Davis around 3:15. Jimmy was home, having taken the day off from his job as a real estate appraiser. At 6-4 and 267 pounds, he is not easy to miss. A balcony overlooks the forest backyard. We sat and talked and at 5:30 we left for Jimmy's health club where we played basketball, Herm and I in a half-court game of "cutthroat" versus Jimmy who lost 10 baskets to 6. We also swam for about an hour in the pool.

After coming home, Jimmy prepared a marinated steak, cooked the rice, and tossed a salad. Despite the tail-wagging Golden Retrievers, named Rascal and Clousseau, we ate a hearty dinner. Tomorrow we plan to go to Blue Lake in Alpine County, not too far from our 1996 trip to Hell-Hole which is aptly named, considering the thick clouds of mosquitoes that descended on us on our first night in camp.

Today we left for Blue Lake on Highway 88, an alternate route to South Shore of Lake Tahoe. Stopped several times for road construction; at one place everyone got out of their cars, trucks, and vans to stretch and eat a sandwich!, then finally reached Highway 89 and went past Silver Lake where I had gone to Scout camp with Napa's Troop 10 in 1957 and 1958 and Coples Lake, et al, until we drove over five miles of dirt road to Blue Lake. Many were fishing from the bank; we proceeded onto a lonely stretch of road, pulled off, and ventured down a hill, baited our hooks using salmon eggs and power bait and fished for about thirty to forty minutes. Not one bite. We decided to leave, drove back through all the fishers we had seen, many of whom had left, and we saw a young brown bear ambling brazenly through the camp. It seemed to be looking for Mama Bear. We took pictures since I had never seen a bear in broad daylight in the Sierras before.

We left Blue Lake and headed toward South Lake Tahoe. Herm wanted to try Markleeville since he had seen a fisherman with a string of fish there before. Markleeville is a quaint hamlet high in the snow country; it is a step back in time. We toured the museum with its replicas of a general store's items; Washoe Indian artifacts; citizenship papers of "Snowshoe" Thompson, a local mail carrier on snowshoes and whose heroic efforts to save and help people have become legendary, along with his snowshoes on the wall; books on California mammals, flowers, and frontiersmen like Kit Carson, a legendary scout, pathfinder, and leader who resided in Taos, New Mexico with his Mexican wife and children. Outside, a model of a log jail next door yields a taste of how jail conditions were over a hundred years ago; dark, somewhat barbarous, remote from the full spectrum of contemporary "due process."

After taking some parting pictures, we journeyed back into town and visited the general store. There was not much that attracted our momentary taste for quaintness. Fishing in the Carson River was not possible simply because our fishing gear was hook-and-bait based, not barbless fly fishing gear. Only Jimmy had a fly fishing outfit but he did not want to fish while Herm and I could not. Catch-and-Release too was not our goal, but that was the law.

Then we drove on to South Lake Tahoe where we spent about forty minutes photographing some houses and one townhouse as part of Jimmy's work as a real estate appraiser. I wrote notes about each property as Jimmy described them as "shagged exterior," "larger unit above garage," and "ugly blue."

After that, it was on to Stateline and Harrah's Club up to the 18th floor for a buffet. Jimmy had three dinners; Herm and I had two. There was enough filet mignon to go around. Overeating is just what "all you can eat" invites you to do. Then back to Pollock Pines and the Gold Ridge Club where we swam for about an hour. When we arrived home, Jimmy's wife, Christina, three weeks from having their first child, a daughter who would be named Alyssa, was home from Danville. It was great to see her again. She was not surprised we had not caught any fish. She called it the "Herrman curse." Just joking, I am sure. She did not want to watch a Pink Panther movie with Peter Sellers as the bumbling sleuth Inspector Clousseau. But we did. *The Pink Panther Strikes Again* was hilarious, especially the dentist scene where Clousseau pulls out one of former Chief Inspector Dreyfuss' incisors instead of his molar. As Dreyfuss says, despite being given laughing gas: "Only one man would pull the wrong tooth. Kill him!"

Next day we woke up at 9:30, drank a cup of hot coffee, ate a poppy seed muffin, and decided to fish PG&E's pond called "El Dorado Forebay." In the hour we fished there, only Herm got three bites on night crawlers. A grandfather and grandson came along, throwing crumbs on the bank and every duck and goose on the pond converged on our fishing spot and ruining what fishing possibilities there were. For lunch, Jimmy suggested a unique hamburger place called the "Del Monte Express" in Camino, California, about seven minutes down the road from Pollock Pines. "Grand View Station" as it is called, cooks a variety of hamburgers which is their specialty. It specializes in burgers very much, but to a lesser extent than, the "Burger Barn" in Cloverdale. Quite a delicious burger! It was already 2 p.m. Herm had promised his wife, Carolyn Jean, he would be home for supper so we decided to head back to Davis and Kenwood, home of the Kenwood Casuals soccer team.

July 26-28, 2002. We arrived in Eureka, a 6 and 1/2 hour trip from Davis. We stopped in Lucerne, a town on the shores of Clear Lake and ate at Foster's Freeze. We then drove on and later stopped in the quaint little town of Garberville where we ate at the Subway Sandwich Shop. On we drove to towns such as Fortuna on our way to Eureka. We could tell we were close to the coast because a thick layer of fog clung to the horizon. We finally arrived in Eureka. As we drove along Broadway, tops of ship masts, hotels, restaurants all stood under an ever-present fog. We ate at Denny's, found no swimming pool, and finally went to our hotel and went to sleep. It was both hot and cold this morning. We had a continental breakfast and watched TV. The kids enjoyed *Scooby Doo*, the *Flinstones*, *Leave it to Beaver*, and the *Donna Reed Show*. So many channels, so few watchable programs. A paucity of good shows; sometimes the best shows were made thirty-five years ago.

The fog in Eureka is a white fog glare still hanging around. Thinking about yesterday's trip, I was impressed by the beauty of Clear Lake with mountains in the background. I had not been to Clear Lake since 1965 when I went waterskiing with a friend, Michael Poggenburg. It convinced me waterskiing was not my sport; doing the splits on skis is not something you want to experience!

Today we visited Humboldt State University where the writer and poet Raymond Carver went to school. I

71

have enjoyed his poems and stories over the years. At the bookstore which is on the top floor of a building with a clock tower which is on the top floor. You have to be a hiker to climb all the stairs. Finally at the building itself there is a glass elevator with a gorgeous view of the Pacific in the distance. Bought a long-sleeved shirt with "Humboldt State Lumberjacks" printed on it. Ricky got a small pee-wee football. Even at moments in the sun, it is hot up there partly because the buildings are clustered together in a somewhat compact campus. As we left the campus, I was delighted that, being so close, I had at least visited the home of the Lumberjacks.

To the Arcata community pool we drove. For $10.50, we paid admission for Ricky, Katie, and me to swim. Rita watched our clothes and read a novel as we swam. Ricky and Katie swam until Katie's goggles broke. I swam eighteen laps in the lane closest to the children's pool. After an hour or so of swimming, we drove back to Eureka and decided to go to the Disney move "Lilo and Stitch." I liked the way it emphasized the importance of family (ahanu in Hawaiian) but found it was a bit contrived.

This morning we got our customary slow start and drove to the Samoa Cook House, once a company-owned community of Samoans on the coast during the rapacious days of an unfettered lumber industry, the early 1900s, and decided to come back for dinner tonight. We drove on to Arcata again north to the once-flourishing whaling town of Trinidad. Down the hill we walked, toward Trinidad State Beach. Instead of arriving there, we had walked from the picnic area to the Humboldt State University marine laboratory. The kids also took a self-guided tour which included everything from trilobites to an octopus, dogfish, sharks, eelgrass, pipe fish, and sea anemones to various species of Rockfish. An unexpected discovery, the way I like to tour. Back to the picnic area: we drove to the Memorial Lighthouse with its plaque of names of those lost at sea. We observed harbor seals on rocks with our binoculars. Then on to the Redwood Acres and Fair: Katie and Ricky got tattoos; Katie a unicorn on her right arm; Ricky a shark on his inner right forearm.

Katie rode a pony twice and the merry-go-round; Ricky won a button at the pig races by answering the question: "When were pigs first introduced into North America?" The answer was 1532? Ricky answered 1692 and got the prize. His answer was close enough to win.

At the fair, Rita won a dolphin for Ricky; I won one for Katie. Ricky also won an alien balloon. Then on to the Samoan Cook House for $12.95 each for Rita and I; $5.95 for kids between ages 8 and 11. We had barbeque pork, roast beef with delicious homemade bread, soup, salad, and apple pie. It was an above average meal and all you can eat. The soup was outstanding. Then we drove back to our hotel where Ricky, Katie, and I sat in the Jacuzzi spa for about fifteen minutes. Then off to the hotel room where Rita showed them how to play poker. It had been a long, exciting day.

This morning we drove to Patrick's Point; it did not this day have much for kids to do so we headed north to Big Lagoon State Park. Down a winding road we went to a boat launch and dock. It was cold with a constant mild breeze. We watched a party of three begin to launch their small sailboat; it looked as though the wind would topple it; they zigzagged back and forth until the boat entered the wider bay and their mast became thinner and thinner until it disappeared in the distance. Awhile later, an inflatable boat on pontoons was launched. It, too, left at 5 mph until out in the wider bay. Meanwhile, Katie and Ricky began fishing with power bait. Between the two of them, they caught seven small fish. They were very happy! Soon a mist began blowing with the wind. As the wind grew stronger, the mist became thicker. After enduring another thirty minutes of this, we decided to go. It was overcast yet we drove north past elk grazing in the meadows, through fog that draped the trees so thickly only headlights, like tiny white eyes shone through the fog. Finally we arrived in Crescent City, victim of a 1964 tsunami, ate at Denny's, drove around, and ventured to the coast with rocks beaten into a surrealscape off shore and large hunks of driftwood that dotted the beach. The lighthouse was a moving experience, a life or death landmark for those at sea. Its revolving beacon was, of course, for ships at sea. On the return trip, we drove through fog-enshrouded forests and watched a herd of elk graze in a meadow. It was a long day, followed by Katie, Ricky, and I soaking in the hotel's Jacuzzi spa.

Today it is sunny and bright, atypical one would imagine for these parts. Drove south on Highway 101 to the "Avenue of the Giants" as part of the Redwood National Forest. Redwoods grow to 300 feet high, can live over 2,000 years, dwarf us, make us stop in a reverential silence, and realize what a tiny blip in time we really are. They tower into the sky. At one stop in the "Avenue of Giants" we saw a redwood that had lived from 1148-1987, through the signing of the Magna Charta (1215), Columbus' re-discovery of the New World (1492), the Declaration of Independence (1776), both world wars, etc. We left the Visitor's Center and drove to a part of the Eel River called "Gould Bar," parked, went to the river where it was too shallow. We moved down river where it got up to above five feet deep. Katie and Ricky fished and fished but not much more than a few nibbles. A bright, sunny glorious day: in the afternoon, periodic breezes that felt so good because it was so hot; with the wind in the pines, the sound of wind on water, of water falling, the occasional creak and sway of redwoods, the chatter of birds in the thick forest groves and glens, it was a mystical closeness to nature I felt. It was wonderful to experience this on this exquisite afternoon.

Prior to our fishing trip, we ate at a place called Sicilito's in Garberville, a combination of Mexican and Italian cuisine. On the walls of this restaurant were all kinds of sports memorabilia. I was impressed by a color photo of Mickey Mantle. Yogi Bera, and Roger Maris. Other sports celebrities included pictures of Babe Ruth with Lou Gehrig; Ernie Nevers of Stanford with his coach "Pop" Warner. It is a wonderful place for those who love collectibles. Then it was off to our home in Davis.

March 29, 2015. The visual artist Richard L. Dana (see his *Le Voyage Fantastique*) and his wife Kitty took us to the

Renaissance Marriott Hotel where we left our bags and later found a parking place and walked over to see the Jefferson and FDR memorials. It was quite windy but not as windy as the day before. Earlier that morning we went to the very busy Original Pancake House and had banana and chocolate chip pancakes along with our omelettes. I had six cups of coffee and a ham and cheese omelette with maple syrup. Then it was onto memorials. We hiked about a mile or so then parked at the Chevy Chase section of southern Maryland to Rosa Mexicano for dinner. I gave two scoops of chocolate ice cream to Rita because I know she loves chocolate.

March 30, 2015. This morning we took a star taxi cab to the Library of Congress. As we approached the library, police waved all of us away since there was a suspicious package in the library. The place was crawling with cops. Rita and I wanted to get out of the swift, cold wind so we went across the street to the Capitol Building. Once inside, after waiting in line, we found the cafeteria. I had a salad, a roast beef sandwich, and some coffee. Rita also had a roast beef sandwich and water. We then entered the long tunnel that took us directly to the Library of Congress. We could not have access to the books without a library card. So we went to the registration room, showed our drivers licenses, were photographed, and given a card with our account number on it. Since Rita had to get to the opening of her business conference, I stayed at the library and looked up books on the Bunch family. One thing I learned was that the Bunch family had been in Virginia since 1642. Around 5:45 Rita and I went to the Panera Bread restaurant for dinner. It had been a full day.

March 31, 2015. Today I slept late. Rita went to her conference which started at 8:30. I went back to sleep since I had the beginning symptoms of a cold. Later, I went to the Carnegie Library to donate a copy of *Plato's Cave* but was told it was a private library, not a public one. Then I went to get some food at the President's Sports Bar in the hotel. I had an Angus burger and salad. Then I went back to sleep until about 3:06. I got up shaved, showered and shampooed. When Rita came back, we went to the Match Box in Chinatown and had pizza. Later, I wrote a poem titled "Inside the Sun" which would later be published in *Lalitamba Magazine* in New York City.

April 1, 2015. Today I went nowhere in particular except to get our Enterprise rental car, a red Nissan Altima with good headroom. Then after somehow enduring one traffic delay after another in D.C. and on Highway 395, we finally arrived at Diamond Hotel Resort. Our only stop was at a Burger King in Lorton, Va. off highway 395. I had a fish sandwich, fries, and Diet Coke. Rita had a chicken sandwich and water. The resort is a gated community with ponds that had Canada geese stroking around on them. It was cold but we wanted to sample outstanding Chinese food so we went to Peter Chang's Restaurant, the one Richard and Kitty told us about. Delicious pancakes, broccoli beef, rice, noodles, potstickers, jumbo shrimp, and sesame chicken: it was the best authentic food as if we were in mainland China. Before it got dark, I took about a ten minute walk. It had been an exhausting day.

April 2, 2015. Today went to Jamestown, Virginia and saw the glass blowing building of 1608. It takes four years to be qualified to work there and to know how to make vases, bottles of all kinds, how to put fluting on the texture of the glass a kiln that can go up to 2,400 degrees Fahrenheit. We bought a small vase. Then we went on to the fort at Jamestown where we saw a model of what it actually looked like. Then we went into the church where my ancestor Pocahontas married John Rolfe. They had a son, Thomas Rolfe, from whom so many are descended. Saw the statue of John Smith and Pocahontas. Then on to the museum of archaeological facts, skeletons of those killed, etc.

The afternoon was spent on the campus of William and Mary College where my mother was accepted for admission but decided to marry my dad instead. Browsed the bookstore but it did not have any of the books I was interested in. Colonial Williamsburg was somewhat disappointing in that people were dressed in colonial attire and it was a nice historical tourist trap for parents who had children who could talk about what they did over vacation. The only thing that interested us was a coach ride pulled by two horses. Unfortunately, it was sold out. So we left. We ate pizza and kabobs at Zoe's Kitchen. Then we went back to the hotel and watched Stanford beat University of Miami and win the National Invitation Tournament in Madison Square Garden in downtown New York City.

April 3, 2015. Today Rita and I left for Portsmouth where my father and mother's families grew up. My father had one brother, E.R. Bunch, who later became consul to the Netherlands representing Arlington in Fairfax County, Virginia and the state of North Carolina. My mother, DeLores Virginia Veal, who also wrote poetry, had six sisters and one brother, Beverly Pennington Veal. He was the youngest in a family of seven women, including his mother. He is now 87 years young and a retired Lt. Colonel in the United States Marines. In his time of service, he first lied about his age, he was only 17, and got into the U.S. Navy during World War II. Then he transferred to the Marine Corps (Semper fi). He served in the Pacific theater in World War II and after that was over went to Mississippi State University on the GI bill. He graduated with a degree in physical education and soon, once the Korean War broke out, was deployed again to the Pacific theater, this time to Korea. In 1961, he was deployed to Cuba when Fidel Castro replaced one dictator with himself as the new Communist one. When the Vietnam War escalated, he was again deployed to the Pacific theater for two tours of duty in Vietnam. In 1971, President Lyndon Johnson conferred upon him the Meritorious Service Medal for dynamic leadership in his years of service.

Even now he gets calls from those who served under him, including those who thought he was the meanest son of a bitch they had ever met. Yet he never, in all of his years of service, failed to go to hospitals to visit his marines who had been injured in battle.

Since Bev had not had breakfast, we assisted Bev to get into our rental car and headed to his favorite restaurant, the Hometown Diner. He had some eggs, bacon, waffles, and coffee. Rita and I both had omelettes. They were deeelicious. My dad must have felt right at home when he finished New Mexico Tech, worked as an apprentice in Norfolk Naval Shipyard, and when he went to work in the foundry at Pearl Harbor in Honolulu (T.H.) in 1935. Between Norfolk, Newport News, and Portsmouth, there are ships, including navy ships and naval hospitals, everywhere.

When I think of Virginia, I think of wars. There's Yorktown where General Cornwallis and the British surrendered to George Washington of the American Continental Army in 1789. There's Appomattox Courthouse where General Robert E. Lee surrendered to U.S. Grant on April 9, 1865. Battles from that war are all over Virginia, including First and Second Manassas, also known as Bull Run, the bombardment of Richmond, capital of the Confederacy, and Chancellorsville where Lee's right hand man, "Stonewall" Jackson was killed. Small wonder then my father, a Virginian, would launch the nuclear submarine Stonewall Jackson at Mare Island Naval Shipyard in Vallejo, California in 1960. Our son Rick has the gold launch key that sent that sub down the ways.

We gave Uncle Bev a UC Davis cap, a copy of my poetry book titled *California Dreaming: Poems of the Golden State*, and an album with pictures of the family: Lani, Carl, me, Rita, Kate, Rick, Graham, Marge, Barry, Rory, Kirstin, Sean Jr. and Maddie Morgan (Rory's children).

Finally, just before three p.m. we said our goodbyes and drove back to our hotel and decided to go to Peter Chang's Chinese restaurant in Williamsburg. We had delicious Scallion Bubble Pancakes with curry sauce, dumplings, Mongolian beef, broccoli chicken, pork chow mein and the list goes on. What a way to end the culinary day with authentic food as it is made in China.

CPSIA information can be obtained
at www.ICGtesting.com
Printed in the USA
FSOW03n1008150716
22726FS